# GARDEN & HOME
## BUILDER

JAN.1926
35 CENTS

F. William
Haemmel

Vol. XLII. No. 5.
Boston     *Doubleday, Page & Company, Garden City, N.Y.*     Chicago

# EVERYTHING
## *for* *the* GARDEN

JUDITH B. TANKARD

**RICHARD C. NYLANDER**

ALAN EMMET

**VIRGINIA LOPEZ BEGG**

HISTORIC NEW ENGLAND

2019

The Rhododendrons.
Country Place of
Professor Charles S. Sargent, Brookline, Mass.
Painted for the Century
by Hobart Nichols.

# Contents

Foreword by Carl R. Nold ❀ 7

Editor's Note by Richard Cheek ❀ 9

Donor Acknowledgments ❀ 11

## Reading the Garden
*Books and Magazines for Green Thumbs* ❀ 13

Judith B. Tankard

## Great Expectations
*A Cornucopia of Catalogues* ❀ 37

Richard C. Nylander

## Beyond the Garden Gate
*Art, Architecture, and Ornament* ❀ 69

Richard C. Nylander

## Where Flowers Never Fade
*Portraits of Older Gardens* ❀ 95

Alan Emmet

## An Unexpected Story
*Social Revolution and the Garden Club* ❀ 125

Virginia Lopez Begg

Selected Readings ❀ Illustration Sources ❀ 136

Index ❀ 141

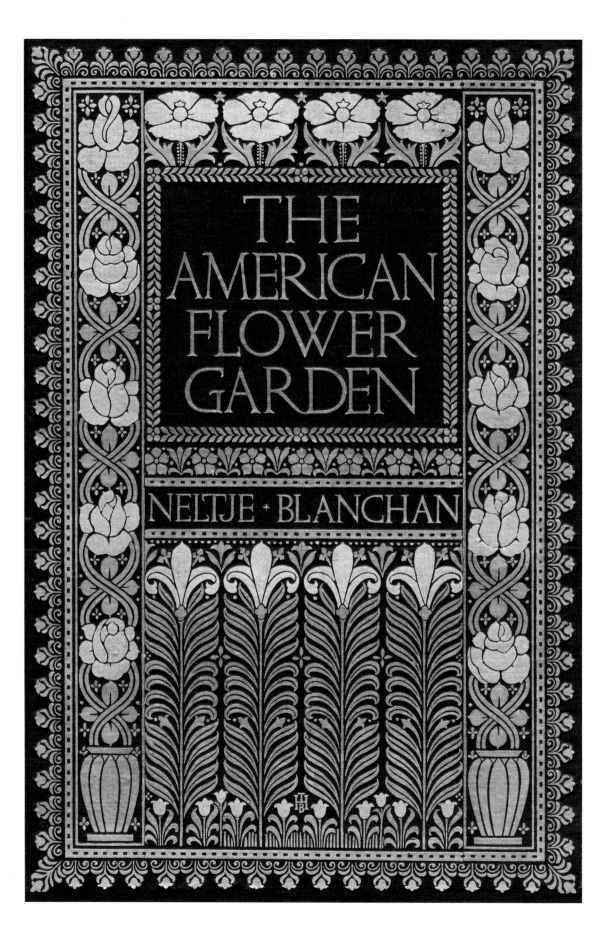

THE AMERICAN FLOWER GARDEN

NELTJE · BLANCHAN

# Foreword

## Carl R. Nold

PRESIDENT AND CEO

We sometimes overlook how frequently the human experience involves interaction with gardens and landscapes, and how significant this is to our well-being. Evolving for centuries from gardens first cultivated for food to include those created entirely for beauty and pleasure, our varied engagements with the land are richly evident in the heritage of New England. The sense of place of this region incorporates its natural and designed landscapes and the variety of gardens found throughout. Recognizing the role of the garden in the region and in our lives, Historic New England has long collected not only the gardens themselves, as parts of our historic site collection, but also documents, images, and artifacts that help tell the stories of New England gardens. The depth and range of these collections prompted this book, which allows us to share with you some

of the remarkable things that have inspired New Englanders' passion for gardens and have been used to craft the physical spaces, develop the designs, acquire the plant materials, and imagine the uses that fill those spaces. One need not be a gardener to find interest in this history, since who among us has not at some time cultivated plants, if only in a small windowsill garden?

These stories could not be told without the dedicated support of our many donors, the leadership of Series Editor Richard Cheek, the contributions of our authors, and the outstanding work of the Historic New England staff, led on this project by Senior Curator of the Library and Archives Lorna Condon. The Historic New England trustees and I are deeply grateful to all who made it possible for us to share with you *Everything for the Garden.*

## MAYFLOWER PREMIUM · Nº 2. 7 ~ FINE BULBS.

I – LILIUM AURATUM —— I – HYACINTHUS CANDICANS — I – GLADIOLUS LEMOINEI
I – LILIUM WALLACEI —— I – GLADIOLUS CHILDSI —— I – MONTBRETIA ——
I – LILIUM DOUBLE TIGER. ALL GIVEN FREE TO EACH SUBSCRIBER. SEE ALSO COVER PAGES

# Editor's Note

Richard Cheek

This book is about the wonderfully elaborate and absorbing process of home gardening in America and its dependence upon myriad how-to books, catalogues, and advertising ephemera that promise to provide "everything for the garden," from information on design and plant selection to tools, clothing, and pink flamingos. Right from the start of the New Republic in 1789, successful gardening had to be a collaborative effort, requiring local supply systems, ingenuity, knowledge sharing, and plenty of hard work.

Imagine yourself as a first-time garden maker today. If you wanted to create a garden in an empty part of your front or backyard, what would you do to get started? You would probably go to the nearest bookstore or library and scout the gardening section, looking for how-to books and manuals. Then you would visit the closest hardware store or plant nursery to begin buying the tools you are told you would need. And before getting down and dirty, you would certainly want to dress the part, acquiring proper gloves, a fashionable sun hat, and a pair of boots to keep the mud out. Depending upon how serious your horticultural ambitions were, you would probably consult plant lists on the Internet before acquiring the seeds or seedlings you decide to plant.

The process of making and maintaining a flower or vegetable garden is a consumer's dream because it provides an endless excuse for shopping sprees via computer or automobile to acquire everything you will need to earn recognition for your green thumb among your neighbors. Every stage in developing and expanding your garden will require additional purchases. For example, all those tools will have to be housed in a shed that will have to be enlarged when you buy a lawn mower that you can ride around on. Also, after you join the local garden club, you will have to add landscape histories to your library to show that you are familiar with all the famous garden styles of the past. And you will want to keep up with current trends by subscribing to garden magazines and by owning the latest surveys of contemporary work by the leading professional designers.

As your garden progresses, you may want to enhance its appeal by adding the sight and sound of a fountain, the shade of a graceful gazebo, the elegance of an entrance gate, or the grace of a sculpted figure terminating a newly paved path. To allow guests to sit or swing as they admire your handiwork, you'll purchase handsome chairs, benches, and a hammock, and for entertaining, you'll have to acquire tables, a drinks cart, and a stainless steel barbecue. You can't tell time on a sunny day without a sundial, and you'll install a mirror globe so you can take old-fashioned selfies of yourself standing amid the blossoms.

You get the picture, I'm sure. The seed for this book was planted by President and CEO Carl R. Nold, who wanted to emphasize the cornucopia of garden books, catalogues, and related ephemera in Historic New England's Library and Archives. It is the fourth volume in our pictorial history series, with five chapters by four distinguished authors. As series editor, I am very grateful to the scholars who so ably described six of the most significant aspects of garden making in America: Judith B. Tankard on garden writing; Richard C. Nylander on commercial catalogues, architecture, and ornament; Alan Emmet on garden portraits; and Virginia Lopez Begg on garden clubs.

### NOTE ON ILLUSTRATIONS

Each chapter has its own set of numbered illustrations, beginning with its frontispiece. When several images appear on a page, they are numbered from left to right and then top to bottom. A central image surrounded by other illustrations within a two-page spread is numbered first, then the rest are numbered clockwise from the upper left. Every image is identified by chapter and number in the Illustration Sources at the back of the book.

# DONOR ACKNOWLEDGMENTS

### GARDEN ANGELS

Anonymous

Richard and Betsy Cheek

Caren and Randy Parker

### HORTICULTURAL HEROES

Lorna Condon

Emily and Frank Hunnewell

In memory of Peggy Kirk

### GARDEN DESIGNERS

Mr. and Mrs. Ralph H. Doering, Jr.

In honor of Joyce E. Jenks, Master Gardener

Carl R. Nold and Vicky L. Kruckeberg

### WORTHY WEEDERS

John M. Carpenter ✿ Mary H. Hohenhaus and John A. Totter

Sidney and Geoffrey Kenyon ✿ Mary H. and Stanley W. Klock

In memory of Joanne Carpenter Landsteiner

### GARDEN GNOMES

In honor of Hope L. Baker ✿ David Berman and Elizabeth Creedon

Lynne Brosch ✿ Daniel Campbell-Benson

In honor of Marcia Corey ✿ Susanna M. Crampton

John C. Doering, Jr. ✿ Orla Blair Doering ✿ Mary Jean Farrington

Leslie A. Frost ✿ Sarah B. Gant

In honor of Elizabeth T. Hain ✿ Elliot Isen

In honor of Jeanne Kent ✿ Maryanne and Julie King

David and Madelyn Kubiak ✿ Robert D. Mussey and Carol Stocker

Katherine Page and Alan Hein ✿ Susan E. Rudd

Yoko and Daniel Sandler ✿ William and Molly Sherden

Thomas D. and Diane Z. Shipp ✿ Caroline F. Sloat

Gary and Diane Viera

## 1

# THE HOUSE BEAUTIFUL

CARROLL BILL

# SUMMER HOUSE NUMBER
# JUNE 1916

25 CENTS $2.00 A YEAR    THE HOUSE BEAUTIFUL PUBLISHING COMPANY, Inc.    3 PARK ST., BOSTON, MASS.

# READING THE GARDEN

## BOOKS AND MAGAZINES FOR GREEN THUMBS

Judith B. Tankard

American gardeners, whether hobbyists or professionally trained designers, have always enjoyed a rich legacy of garden literature to consult. From nurserymen's guides such as Bernard M'Mahon's 1806 *The American Gardener's Calendar* to the still popular how-to series *Taylor's Weekend Gardening Guides* initiated in the 1990s, plenty of advice was at the fingertips of gardeners regardless of the size of their home grounds or their budgets.

For families that were leaving congested cities in favor of the pleasures of country life in the late nineteenth and early twentieth centuries, the literature was particularly rich. There was endless information available on home building, garden making, and reaping the benefits of healthful outdoor living. Whether they lived in the suburbs or one of the new garden cities, in an Arts and Crafts bungalow or a grand Colonial, homeowners mainly looked to books and periodicals for ideas on garden making.

Around 1900 a flurry of popular books about American gardens and their history, written primarily by women, began to educate a new generation of gardeners. Social historian Alice Morse Earle's book, *Old Time Gardens Newly Set Forth* (1901), presented a nostalgic view of colonial gardens as a starting point for using old-fashioned flowers and garden furnishings to create a romantic garden evocative of yesteryear. She followed this book with *Sun-Dials and Roses of Yesterday* (1902), the sundial being a key ornamental element in many New England gardens. Such gardens represented a romanticized vision of the colonial era and were seen as a delightful antidote to Victorian gardens laid out in rigid geometry and filled with a jarring assemblage of short-lived annuals.

Books with a more practical bent balanced that nostalgic approach, such as Helena Rutherfurd Ely's *A Woman's Hardy Garden* (1904), which helped to create a special niche for women as gardeners. In *The Garden Month by Month* (1907), New Englander Mabel Cabot Sedgwick was among the first to produce a practical handbook for the home gardener on the art of maintaining perpetual bloom in the garden. As her subtitle states, the book describes "the appearance, color, dates of bloom, height and cultivation of all desirable Hardy Herbaceous Perennials." Neltje Blanchan's lavishly illustrated *The American Flower Garden* (1909) included chapters ranging from general design advice to the specifics of wild gardens, rock gardens, water gardens, trees and shrubs, and more. It, too, was a standard resource for women who were now meeting the challenges of gardening on their own, as viewed with humor and lightheartedness in Mabel Osgood Wright's pseudonymous classic, *The Garden of a Commuter's Wife* (1901).

Paralleling the popularization of gardening for women was the emergence of the profession of landscape architecture, thanks to Frederick Law Olmsted's career. The founding of the American Society of Landscape Architects in 1899 as well as the establishment of the landscape architecture program at Harvard University in 1900 were important landmarks. Since women were denied entrance to the all-male program at Harvard, several schools were founded in the early 1900s to train women for careers in garden design. Influenced by the spread of the system of architectural education and practice developed at the École des Beaux-Arts in Paris, increased emphasis was placed on the study of historic styles and their principles of design, rational planning, and apprenticeship with a master practitioner after graduation. One of the first writers to stir interest among women in this field was Mariana Griswold Van Rensselaer, an architectural critic who brought aristocratic recognition to gardening arts in her book, *Art Out-of-Doors: Hints on Good Taste in Gardening* (1893). She defined the landscape gardener as "a gardener, an engineer, and an artist, who like an architect considers beauty and utility together."

By the turn of the twentieth century, growing wealth in America allowed many magnates to hire these professionally trained architects and landscape architects to design grand estates rivaling English country houses, French *chateaux,* Italian villas, and Spanish plantations. A flurry of large, lavishly illustrated monographs on historic garden styles in European countries was produced, opening up a new world of ideas for architects as well as home designers. Many hefty tomes featuring these palatial mansions were also published, such as Guy Lowell's *American Gardens* (1902) and Barr Ferree's *American Estates and Gardens* (1904).

By emphasizing the aesthetic dimension, Van Rensselaer may have inspired the noted landscape gardener Beatrix Farrand, who easily combined an artist's eye for design with a deep knowledge of horticulture (which she acquired in private studies at Harvard's Arnold Arboretum), to take up a profession then dominated by men. Farrand as well as her colleagues wrote articles on garden design for home and garden publications or had their projects published in them. In 1910, for example, Farrand published an article on "Laying Out a Suburban Place" in *Country Life in America.* For a small lot (less than half an acre), she advised "getting as large an open space near the living room windows as is possible," while disdaining the usual "scattered masses of shrubbery" that would only look crowded and not give the illusion of space. Although Farrand rarely publicized her own work, many of her colleagues, such as Ellen Shipman and Marian Coffin, did. Shipman's gardens were regularly featured in *The Garden Magazine,* one of many periodicals during the golden age of American magazines in the early 1900s that were devoted to homes and gardens. They featured luscious illustrations and dazzling covers designed by leading artists of the day. Among the best were *American Homes and Gardens, House & Garden, The House Beautiful, Country Life in America* (modeled after the English *Country Life*), and *The Ladies' Home Journal,* as well as *The Garden Magazine* (later *Garden & Home Builder*). For specialists, Elbert Hubbard's *The Craftsman* appealed to owners of smaller Arts and Crafts bungalows with their old-fashioned flower gardens.

Further examples of distinguished gardens designed by women were published in surveys, such as Louise Shelton's 1915 *Beautiful Gardens in America,* which she updated in 1924. Hers was one of the first books to shift the emphasis from horticulture to garden aesthetics, discussing both historic and new gardens all over the country. It was illustrated by the leading garden photographers of the day, including Mattie Edwards Hewitt and Frances Benjamin Johnston, and it inspired thousands of home gardeners about design, scale, and planting.

It is impossible to talk about the progress of American garden design without referring to the influence of English gardening books. While many in the United States were continuing to set out garishly planted geometrically shaped beds of flowers around houses in the 1860s, the appearance of William Robinson's *The Wild Garden* in 1870 introduced new generations of gardeners to the merits of native plants used in naturalistic settings as a complement to formal flower borders. Robinson's *The English Flower Garden* (1883), a perennial favorite still in print today, promoted ideas that were augmented by his colleague, Gertrude Jekyll. Illustrated with her own photographs of her garden at Munstead Wood in Surrey, England, Jekyll's book, *Colour in the Flower Garden* (1908), advised that one should devote certain borders to certain times of year, each border to be of interest for a limited period of time. A series of subsequent books became very popular with American readers, especially those titles that dealt with designing and installing gardens for both new and old English country houses. Jekyll's insistence on color harmony in the garden would be echoed by many American garden writers, particularly by Louise Beebe Wilder in her popular book, *Colour in My Garden* (1918).

Although consulting with a professional designer might be the most efficient way to start a new garden, most first-time gardeners seem to prefer to make the best of it on their own. One of the books that has worked well in the past for dealing with the dilemma of personally creating a garden was Grace Tabor's popular *The Landscape Gardening Book*, published in 1911 and still available. As she stated in her introduction, "Gardens do not happen. A Garden is as much the expression of an idea as a poem, a symphony, an essay—a subway, an office-building or a gown!" In the book, which is devoted to the practicalities of garden making rather than gardening, Tabor recommends going slowly, practicing self-denial, and understanding that "everything will not go into one garden."

Nevertheless, for those too impatient to follow Tabor's advice, there has always been a desire to obtain some form of all-in-one publication that will tell them everything they need to know or have, from garden plans and plant lists to tools and best methods to follow when tending the garden. There have been many attempts to provide this ideal cornucopia of information: a one-volume encyclopedia in the late eighteenth century, the nurseryman's planting calendar; a mid-twentieth century notebook with updatable tab sections, *Better Homes and Gardens Garden Book*; and Houghton Mifflin's fifteen-volume series, *Taylor's Weekend Gardening Guides*, started in the 1990s and still selling.

Today the passion for gardening is as vibrant as ever, with many gardeners turning to some of the older classics on the subject as well as new publications focusing on contemporary designers, regional gardens, and new plants for specific climates. Even though today's information is readily available on the Internet, the old-fashioned pleasures of thumbing through catalogues and how-to publications still exist, along with modern books whose lush color photography captivates all levels of gardeners and garden lovers.

2

THE
# AMERICAN GARDENER'S CALENDAR;
ADAPTED
TO THE CLIMATES AND SEASONS
OF THE
## UNITED STATES.
CONTAINING
A COMPLETE ACCOUNT OF ALL THE WORK NECESSARY TO BE DONE IN THE

KITCHEN-GARDEN,    PLEASURE-GROUND,
FRUIT-GARDEN,    FLOWER-GARDEN,
ORCHARD,    GREEN-HOUSE,
VINEYARD,    HOT-HOUSE, and
NURSERY,    FORCING FRAMES,

FOR EVERY MONTH IN THE YEAR;
*WITH AMPLE PRACTICAL DIRECTIONS*
FOR PERFORMING THE SAME.
ALSO,
General as well as minute instructions, for laying out, or erecting, each and every of the above departments, according to modern taste and the most approved plans; the ORNAMENTAL PLANTING OF PLEASURE-GROUNDS, in the ancient and modern stile; the cultivation of THORN-QUICKS and other plants suitable for LIVE HEDGES, with the best methods of making them, &c.

TO WHICH ARE ANNEXED,
Extensive CATALOGUES of the different kinds of plants, which may be cultivated either for use or ornament in the several departments, or in rural economy; divided into eighteen separate alphabetical classes, according to their habits, duration, and modes of culture; with explanatory introductions, marginal marks, and their true *Linnean* or *Botanical*, as well as English names; together with a copious *Index* to the body of the work.

BY BERNARD M'MAHON,
NURSERY, SEEDSMAN, AND FLORIST.

PHILADELPHIA:
PRINTED BY B. GRAVES, NO. 40, NORTH FOURTH-STREET,
FOR THE AUTHOR.
1806.

Drawn by A.J Davis.

---

## WINSHIPS' ESTABLISHMENT.

The MESSRS. WINSHIP have the greatest variety of Fruit, Forest, Ornamental Trees, Flowering Shrubs, Herbaceous and Green-house Plants, to be found in the country.

ALL orders forwarded by mail will be executed with promptness, or plants may be selected by persons visiting the Nurseries.
*Brighton, April* 1, 1838.

---

### FRUIT TREES, ORNAMENTAL TREES, MORUS MULTICAULIS, &c.
FOR SALE BY
## WILLIAM KENRICK,
NONANTUM HILL, NEWTON.

The varieties, particularly of the Pears and the Plums were never before so fine, the assortment so complete. Also of Apples, Peaches, Cherries, Grape Vines, a superior assortment of the finest kinds, and of all other hardy fruits.

20,000 Morus Multicaulis, or Chinese Mulberry trees, can still be furnished at the customary prices, if applied for early, this being all that now remains unsold.

Ornamental Trees and Shrubs, Roses and Herbaceous Plants, of the most beautiful hardy kinds. Splendid Pæonies and Double Dahlias.

4,000 Cockspur Thorns, 10,000 Buckthorns for Hedges.

800 Lancashire Gooseberries, of various colors and fine kinds.

Harrison's Double Yellow Roses, new and hardy, color fine, it never fails to bloom profusely.

Trees packed in the most perfect manner for all distant places and shipped or sent from Boston to wherever ordered.

Transportation to the city without charge.

Address by mail post paid.

Catalogues will be sent gratis to those who apply.

---

## CHARLESTOWN VINEYARD.
(*Corner of Eden Street, Charlestown, Mass.*)
### THOMAS MASON,

Keeps a general assortment of Green-house Plants—with a choice collection of Strawberries, Raspberries, Currants, &c.

He offers for sale a quantity of his Seedling Grape Raspberries, which have been pronounced of superior quality.

Orders may be left with Joseph Breck & Co. 51 and 52 North Market Street, Boston.

## T. BRIDGEMAN,
GARDEN, GREENHOUSE AND SEED STORE,
*Corner of Eighteenth Street, Broadway,*
IMMEDIATELY NORTH OF UNION PLACE,
*And West of the New York and Harlem Rail Road,*
NEW YORK.

---

## POMOLOGICAL GARDENS,
SALEM, MASSACHUSETTS.
---
### FRUIT TREES, VINES, SHRUBS,
AND
ORNAMENTAL TREES,
Warranted correct, constantly for sale, at the Pomological Garden of
## ROBERT MANNING,
*Dearborn Street, Salem,*
And at JOHN M. IVES' adjoining NURSERY—packed for transportation, and at Nursery prices.
SCIONS OF FRUIT TREES, &c.

---

## EDWARD SAYERS,
*Landscape & Ornamental Gardener,*
BOSTON, MASS.

*The Erection of Green Houses, Laying out Flower Gardens, Ornamental Planting, &c. designed and superintended.*

Reference, JOSEPH BRECK & Co.
*Agricultural Warehouse,* 51 & 52 *North Market street.*

☞ All letters of communication must be post paid.

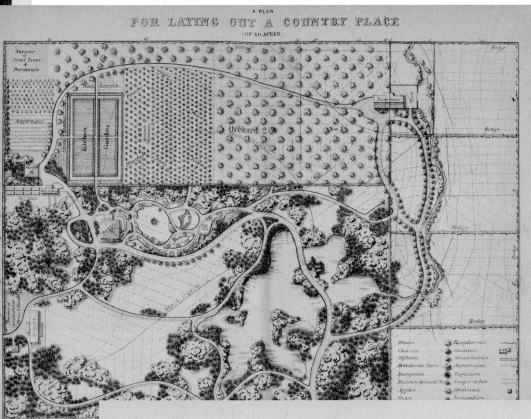

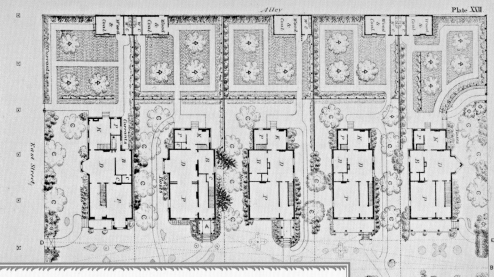

Beginning in the early nineteenth century, garden advice became increasingly available in "calendars" published by nurserymen such as Bernard M'Mahon. By midcentury, Andrew Jackson Downing's popular books (4) and Robert Copeland's *Country Life* (6) were offering guidance on how to lay out estates in scenic locations. **FOLLOWING PAGES:** Most of the popular gardening books published from 1900 through 1918 were written by women. Helena Rutherfurd Ely's *A Woman's Hardy Garden* and Alice Morse Earle's *Old Time Gardens* joined Celia Thaxter's earlier book, *An Island Garden* (see pages 94, 96), as best sellers. Mabel Cabot Sedgwick's practical book, *The Garden Month by Month* (1907), was the first to include a color chart of hardy plants.

OVERLEAF: 8–27 >

A·WOMAN'S
HARDY·GARDEN

HELENA·RUTHERFURD·ELY

FLOWER
GARDENING

HOW TO LAY OUT
SUBURBAN HOME
GROUNDS

OLD TIME
GARDENS
ALICE·MORSE·EARLE

THE GARDEN of a
COMMUTER'S
WIFE

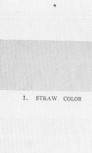

| 1. STRAW COLOR | 8. PUMPKIN ORANGE | 15. PINKISH ORANGE | 22. LIGHT SALMON PINK |
| 2. LEMON YELLOW | 9. ORANGE | 16. NEUTRAL ORANGE VERMILION | 23. ROSE PINK |
| 3. PRIMROSE | 10. NEUTRAL ORANGE | 17. ORANGE VERMILION | 24. DEEP ROSE PINK | 31. |
| 4. SULPHUR YELLOW | 11. DEEP ORANGE | 18. SCARLET VERMILION | 25. OLD ROSE | 32. |
| 5. GAMBOGE YELLOW | 12. RED ORANGE | 19. ORANGE SCARLET | 26. CARMINE PINK |
| 6. GOLDEN YELLOW | 13. BURNT ORANGE | 20. CARDINAL RED | 27. ROSE RED |
| 7. ORANGE YELLOW | 14. TERRA-COTTA | 21. CHOCOLATE | 28. RUBY RED |

A CHART SHOWING THE

THE
LANDSCAPE GARDENING
BOOK

GRACE TABOR

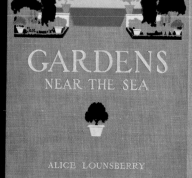

GARDENS
NEAR THE SEA

ALICE LOUNSBERRY

AMATEUR
GARDENCRAFT
BY
EBEN E. REXFORD

THE SEASONS IN A
FLOWER GARDEN
A
HANDBOOK
FOR THE
AMATEUR
BY
LOUISE SHELTON

PINK  36. PALE LIGHT PINK

43. PALE LILAC

50. PALE LILAC BLUE

57. PALE SKY BLUE

NTA  37. DULL LAVENDER PINK

44. PALE BLUE VIOLET

51. AZURE

58. TURQUOISE BLUE

38. MAGENTA PINK

45. DEEP LAVENDER

52. PORCELAIN BLUE

59. DEEP TURQUOISE BLUE

PINK 39. DEEP HELIOTROPE

46. BRIGHT VIOLET BLUE

53. DULL VIOLET BLUE

60. PEACOCK BLUE

40. PURPLE MAGENTA

47. PURPLE VIOLET

54. SAPPHIRE

61. PRUSSIAN BLUE

41. DULL MAROON PURPLE

48. PURPLE

55. BRILLIANT VIOLET

62. PURE BLUE

42. MAROON PURPLE

49. DEEP PURPLE VIOLET

56. DEEP DULL VIOLET BLUE

63. GENTIAN BLUE

## ORS OF GARDEN FLOWERS

The GARDEN YOU AND I

By the Author of "The Garden of a Commuter's Wife"

SUN-DIALS AND ROSES OF YESTERDAY

ALICE MORSE EARLE

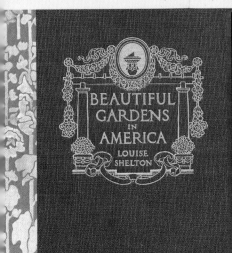

BEAUTIFUL GARDENS IN AMERICA
LOUISE SHELTON

The JOY of GARDENS

LENA MAY McCAULEY

FOUR SEASONS IN THE GARDEN
BY
EBEN E. REXFORD

The GARDEN BOOK of CALIFORNIA

BELLE SUMNER ANGIER

AMERICAN GARDENS

EDITED BY GUY LOWELL

FIFTH STREETS
DELPHIA

April Twenty-eighth
Nineteen Twenty-one

Messrs. Lewis & Valentine,

Ardmore, Pennsylvania.

Dear Sirs:

I am in receipt of your letter o
the 16th, and it gives me great pleasure to s
that the work which you have done for me at
Chestnut Hill has been most satisfactory.

Hoping that you will be able to
cure additional work, I am

Yours very truly,

E. T. Stotesbury

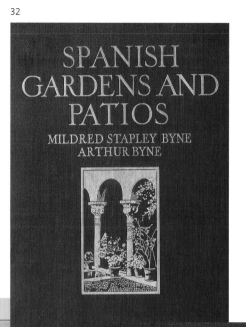

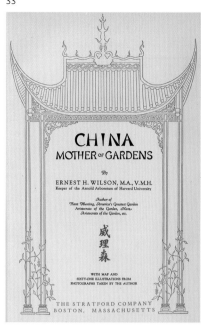

The above is the largest and considered the finest garden built in America
decade. It was planted from our stock of large trees, which gave it imme
ent mature appearance.

*Landscape Planting by Lewis & Valentine Company*

Two lavishly illustrated books, Barr Ferree's *American Estates and Gardens* (1904) and Guy Lowell's *American Gardens* (1902), were among those titles celebrating the grand new estates that reflected Mariana Van Rensselaer's call for greater artistic expression in landscape design in her book *Art Out-of-Doors*. In addition to English, French, and Italian inspirations, Spanish and Asian gardens had also become well known, and Ernest Wilson's *China: Mother of Gardens* had educated gardeners about the value of Asian plants.

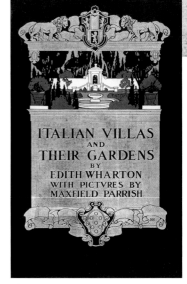

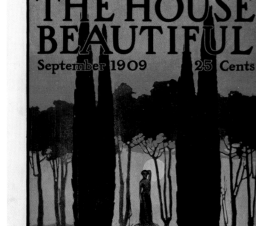

THE·GARDENS OF·ITALY CHARLES LATHAM

ITALIAN GARDENS C·A·PLATT

39

40

41

The pleasures of Italian gardens provided design inspiration for new American estates. The architect Charles Platt's *Italian Gardens* (1894) and Edith Wharton's seminal *Italian Villas and Their Gardens* (1904) with illustrations by Maxfield Parrish enlightened garden architects as well as home gardeners, while Charles Latham's majestic *The Gardens of Italy* (1905) was aimed at garden connoisseurs.

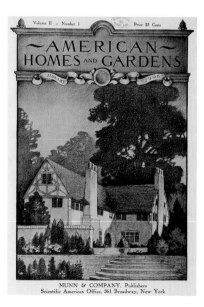

THE HOUSE BEAUTIFUL

GARDEN NUMBER
MARCH 1916

CARROLL BILL

25 CENTS  $2.00 A YEAR        PARK ST., BOSTON, MASS.

The popularity of historically styled residences and gardens being constructed in suburban and country locations was reflected by a great burst of new periodicals. By 1910 there were more
than a dozen American home and garden magazines resting on
upper- and middle-class coffee tables, with *The House Beautiful, House & Garden, Country Life in America,* and *The Ladies'
Home Journal* among the top choices.

52

53

54

At the turn of the twentieth century, books on English gardens whetted the appetites of American gardeners, especially William Robinson's *The Wild Garden* (52), which advocated the use of native plants as opposed to bedded-out annuals, and Gertrude Jekyll's many titles that included practical advice based on years of gardening at Munstead Wood, her home in Surrey, England (54).

55

THE OLD SOUTH WALL.

WHAT ENGLAND CAN TEACH
US ABOUT GARDENING

BY WILHELM MILLER

56

ENGLISH PLEASVRE
GARDENS

ROSE STANDISH NICHOLS

57

GARDENS
OLD AND
NEW

58

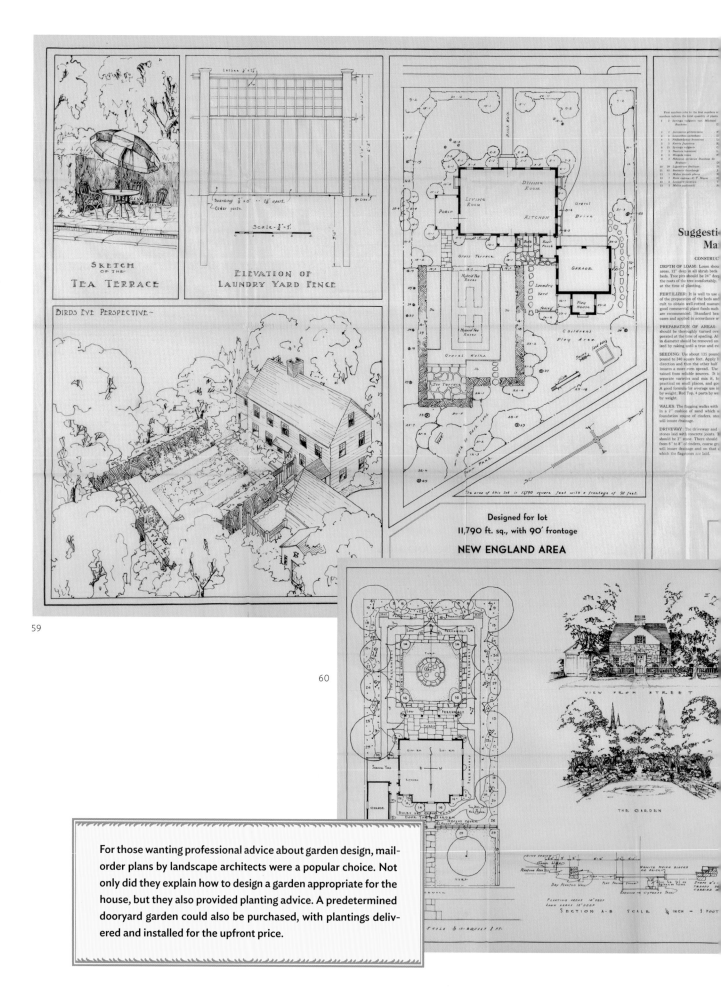

SKETCH OF THE TEA TERRACE

ELEVATION OF LAUNDRY YARD FENCE

BIRDS EYE PERSPECTIVE

Designed for lot
11,790 ft. sq., with 90' frontage

**NEW ENGLAND AREA**

59

60

THE GARDEN

For those wanting professional advice about garden design, mail-order plans by landscape architects were a popular choice. Not only did they explain how to design a garden appropriate for the house, but they also provided planting advice. A predetermined dooryard garden could also be purchased, with plantings delivered and installed for the upfront price.

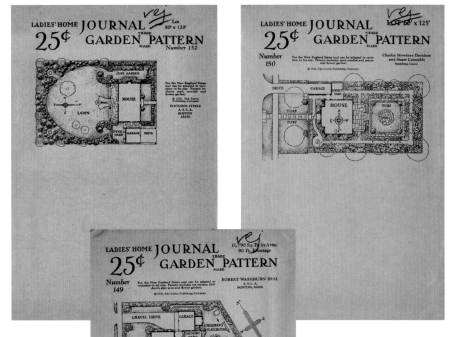

The above planting costs $250 delivered and planted on your property with our guarantee, consists of 2 Cedar trees, 15 ft. high, 2 Arbor-vitae, 6-8 ft. high, 50 large Flowering Shrubs of 10 different varieties, and 50 old-fashioned flowers of different varieties, including Paeonies, Phlox, Iris, Hollyhocks, Lily of the Valley, Anemone, and any others you select.

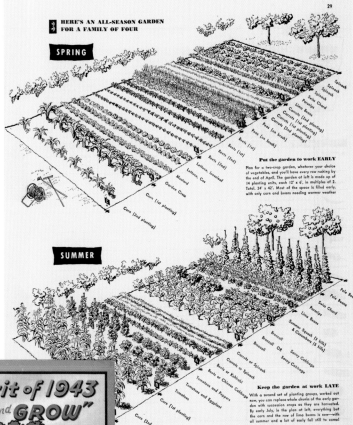

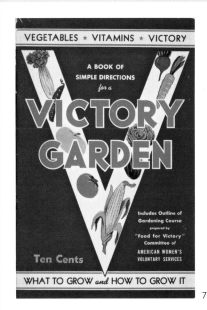

71

Colorful and patriotic books and pamphlets devoted to Victory Gardens flourished during the two world wars. Adults and children alike were encouraged to plant vegetable gardens in any available plot and to harvest the results. Plenty of advice was available, from growing pumpkins and potatoes to strawberries and tomatoes.

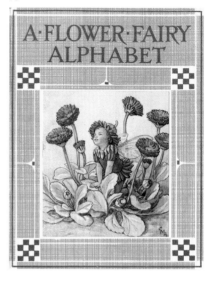

A·FLOWER·FAIRY
ALPHABET

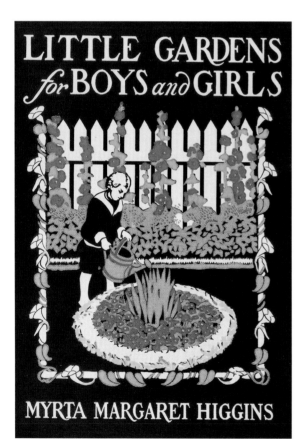

LITTLE GARDENS
for BOYS and GIRLS

MYRTA MARGARET HIGGINS

74

Iris

75

Part of the appeal of family gardens is their educational value for children. As Frances Hodgson Burnett's *The Secret Garden* (1911) demonstrated, a garden can provide a realm of enchantment that spurs imagination, encourages emotional growth, and enhances digital dexterity.

THE SECRET
GARDEN
BY FRANCES
HODGSON BURNETT
ILLUSTRATED BY
CHARLES ROBINSON

WILLIAM HEINEMANN
21 BEDFORD STREET
LONDON · W·C·

### Handbooks of Practical Gardening

Under the General Editorship of
HARRY ROBERTS
Crown 8vo.  With Illustrations
Cloth, 2s. 6d. net.

*The World* says :—" This very useful series should by no means be missed from the library of the sincere gardener."

Vol.
I. THE BOOK OF ASPARAGUS.
   By CHARLES ILOTT, F.R.H.S.
II. THE BOOK OF THE GREENHOUSE.
   By J. C. TALLACK, F.R.H.S.
III. THE BOOK OF THE GRAPE.
   By H. W. WARD, F.R.H.S.
IV. THE BOOK OF OLD FASHIONED FLOWERS.
   By HARRY ROBERTS.
V. THE BOOK OF BULBS.
   By S. ARNOTT, F.R.H.S.
VI. THE BOOK OF THE APPLE.
   By H. H. THOMAS.
VII. THE BOOK OF VEGETABLES.
   By GEORGE WYTHES, V.M.H.
VIII. THE BOOK OF ORCHIDS.
   By W. H. WHITE, F.R.H.S.
IX. THE BOOK OF THE STRAWBERRY.
   By EDWIN BECKETT, F.R.H.S.
X. THE BOOK OF CLIMBING PLANTS.
   By S. ARNOTT, F.R.H.S.
XI. THE BOOK OF PEARS AND PLUMS.
   By the Rev. E. BARTRUM, D.D.
XII. THE BOOK OF HERBS.
   By Lady ROSALIND NORTHCOTE.
XIII. THE BOOK OF THE WILD GARDEN.
   By S. W. FITZHERBERT.
XIV. THE BOOK OF THE HONEY BEES.
   By CHARLES HARRISON.
XV. THE BOOK OF SHRUBS.
   By GEORGE GORDON.
XVI. THE BOOK OF THE DAFFODIL.
   By the Rev. S. EUGENE BOURNE.
XVII. THE BOOK OF THE LILY.
   By W. GOLDRING.
XVIII. THE BOOK OF TOPIARY.
   By W. GIBSON.

JOHN LANE :  LONDON: VIGO STREET, W.
             NEW YORK: 67 FIFTH AVENUE.

83

Basic information
keyed to your area
with a compass rose

Pacific NW    Mt. States    Central-East
California
Texas-SW    South-SE
Florida

Throughout this book the information and all methods given are basic. In addition, items of special interest and service to those gardening in the various regional climates within the United States are indicated on the bordering margins by the compass rose (see above).

If not specified otherwise, directions may be followed with little or no modification through the Central-East.

Seven regions are served here as defined on the map above. The boundaries are not sharp. Altitude, nearness to mountains, proximity of the sea or one of the large lakes, and special soil conditions can all bring about deviations from what is average and good gardening practice within one of these large regions.

For these deviations from average, readers will have to allow, and make certain adjustments in timing and in planting directions.

**Better Homes** and Gardens **Garden Book**

Second Edition
Copyright 1951, 1954
Meredith Publishing Company
Des Moines, Iowa
All rights reserved under the International and Pan-American Conventions. Printed in the United States of America

84

**TAYLOR'S WEEKEND GARDENING GUIDES**

*The Cutting Garden*

Plants for gorgeous bouquets all year long

ROB PROCTOR

**TAYLOR'S WEEKEND GARDENING GUIDES**

*The Winter Garden*

Plants that offer color and beauty in every season of the year

RITA BUCHANAN

TAYLOR'S WEEKEND GARDENING

*Small Gardens*

How to get the most impact from the le

GLENN MORRIS

*The* HOME GARDEN

January 1946

Better Homes & Gardens

Garden Book

A year-round guide to practical home gardening

Lot planning 1

Lawns 2

Continuous bloom 3

Shrubs 5

Evergreens 6

The modern parallel to the nineteenth-century nurseryman's planting calendar is the garden series, which can come in three forms: a monthly magazine, a notebook with tab sections that can be updated, or a multivolume series of how-to books. The last solution is the current method of choice, as represented by Houghton Mifflin's popular *Taylor's Weekend Gardening Guides,* with each volume written by an expert and devoted to a single aspect of gardening.

# GREAT EXPECTATIONS

## A CORNUCOPIA OF CATALOGUES

Richard C. Nylander

In the bleak days of the early new year in New England nothing brightens gardeners' spirits more than the colorful seed and garden catalogues that begin to arrive and tempt them with visions of more verdant seasons ahead. Whether experienced or beginner, gardeners are lured by images of beautiful flowers, lush vegetables, and a vast array of products that will help them achieve the best possible results. Produced in ever-increasing quantities since the mid-nineteenth century, garden catalogues are both practical—giving us "how to" knowledge—and inspirational—allowing us to dream a bit.

A look through garden catalogues from several time periods can give us many different avenues to explore, such as the history of seed production and the introduction of new varieties; improvements in methods of cultivation and labor-saving tools and machines; changing styles of planting and landscaping; and an endless assortment of garden ornaments and accessories, both large and small and useful and useless. As we shall see, garden catalogues and related ephemera can also take us on an often nostalgic journey through the popular imagery and graphic styles of times past.

The most familiar catalogues are the seed and nursery offerings that provide the garden's basic plant material, be it for food production or ornamental value. In their earliest form such catalogues were often just single-page lists of plant names with their prices, the kinds that were familiar to George Washington and Thomas Jefferson. Multipage catalogues became more prevalent in the 1840s and 1850s. More than one was titled *A Descriptive Catalogue* because they included additional information such as the plant's common and scientific names, its characteristics and blooming time, and cultivation notes, much like today's catalogues.

Separate catalogues were published for flowers and vegetables, the latter often including fruit trees and vines. At first few were illustrated, and then with only one or two line engravings. Better-illustrated catalogues became more widespread after the Civil War and by the 1880s some featured colorful and enticing covers and plant portraits. These were the result of advances in printing. Chromolithography, printing in color with a series of stones or plates, had been invented about 1837. It was an expensive process at first, but as it became more affordable it was used for mass-produced items like posters, greeting cards, and the advertising trade cards that became ubiquitous in the 1880s and 1890s. Many of the seed suppliers that are still household names today, such as Breck's, W. Atlee Burpee, Charles C. Hart, and Park Seed, quickly took advantage of this inexpensive color printing process for their catalogues, hoping to attract their competitions' customers.

Seed packets also began to be printed in color in the 1880s. The idea of packaging seeds in individual packets for convenience started in the early nineteenth century and is credited to the Shakers, who were well known for their reliable seeds. They sold their assortments in what are now highly collectible boxes with printed labels. Today, reproductions of these boxes are available in catalogues. As early as 1837, Joseph Breck, who ran a nursery in Brighton, Massachusetts, advertised in a Boston newspaper: "Traders supplied with seeds in boxes as usual." These, like the Shakers' seeds, were transported and sold to country stores for further distribution. Later in the 1850s some Boston purveyors sold collections of "Assorted Seeds for Families" (meaning everything a family would need for a basic kitchen garden, not as some might interpret today, a children's garden starter kit for family fun and education) and even seeds for the West Indies trade. Many companies continued to package their seeds in attractively printed boxes well into the early twentieth century to sell to general and hardware stores that served retail customers.

Seed catalogues were only the beginning of an industry that has produced a profusion of printed matter offering everything imaginable for the garden from flowerpots to giant resin snails. In any number of catalogues gardeners can find every kind of tool they might need for cultivation and maintenance, as well as numerous methods to provide water for the plants to grow, specialized fertilizers to make them flourish and grow larger, and pesticides to keep them free of insects. And then there are catalogues with all the right accessories for any well-outfitted gardener: tubs to hold weeds, trugs for freshly picked flowers and produce, colorful hats to protect the head and gloves for the hands, along with specialized garden gifts "for him and for her."

What is most appealing about many garden catalogues and ephemera are the graphics and illustrations. While some are just straightforward images of the products, others exhibit the artistic conventions of the period in which they were produced. Some of the most imaginative date to the 1880s, when stylized forms and decorative motifs were drawn from the vocabulary of the Aesthetic Movement, children and inanimate objects alike were shown dressed in the old-fashioned style popularized by children's book author and illustrator Kate Greenaway, and vegetables were imbued with human attributes.

Catalogues can also convey ideas through their imagery. Cover illustrations from the 1920s and 1930s promote the suburban ideal that many sought: a well-maintained house, often in the Colonial Revival style, with window boxes and foundation plantings, a brick walk from the front door, and a yard enclosed with a fence. Beautifying the home and its surroundings is a predominant theme during this period and more than one company used the slogan, "It's not a home until it is planted." This is also the time when the American obsession with the perfectly manicured and weed-free lawn began. The backyard could now become an outdoor living room, complete with appropriate lawn furniture and a swing set and a sandbox for the children—all available through catalogues.

Garden catalogues of the twenty-first century respond to a different lifestyle. Preplanted pots are offered to the busy customer who has only a balcony instead of a backyard to "cultivate" and wants instant results. Plant combinations for specific areas of the garden—sunny, shady, or soggy—and collections of color coordinated bulbs are convenient but take the place of the gardener's accumulated knowledge and much of the fun out of experimentation.

In today's digital world the printed catalogue in many cases is being replaced with the online catalogue. Indeed, using the Internet may be a more convenient way to order but nothing can take the place of sitting down and savoring the first catalogue that arrives in the mail at the beginning of each year.

5

RICE'S SEEDS

HAVE SPOKEN THEIR OWN PRAISE WHER-EVER PLANTED FOR *UPWARDS OF 40 YEARS*.

MAYER, MERKEL & OTTMANN LITH. N.Y.

"GREAT EXPECTATIONS."

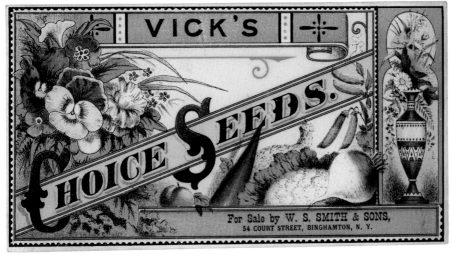

VICK'S

CHOICE SEEDS.

For Sale by W. S. SMITH & SONS,
54 COURT STREET, BINGHAMTON, N. Y.

6

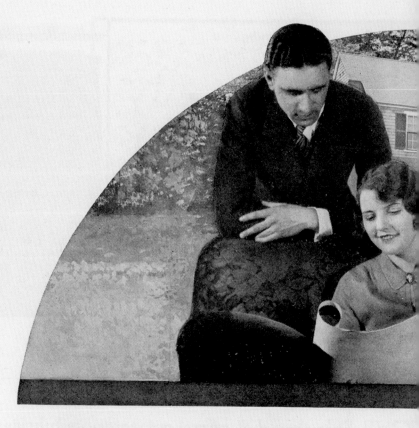

PLANNING A

# D PLANTING

The Book ~ of
Lawn Furniture

J. W. WHITE COMPANY
45-47 Lincoln St.
LEWISTON, MAINE

*ing*

UNDS

| GATES |
| PAGES 4-5 |
| FENCES |
| PAGES 6-7-8 & 9 |
| ARBORS AND ARCHES |
| PAGES 10-11 |
| FURNITURE |
| PAGES 12-13-14 & 15 |
| TRELLISES AND PERGOLAS |
| PAGES 16-17-18-19 & 20 |

ASSOCIATION
EANS

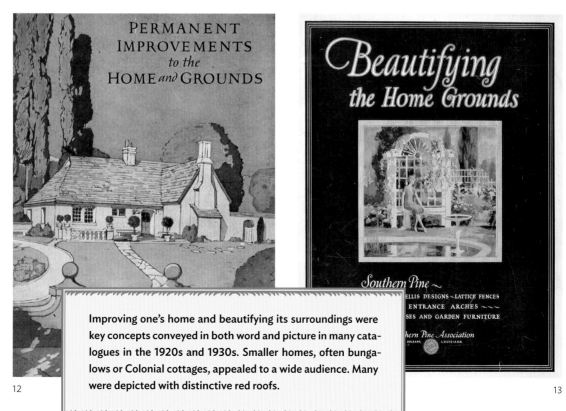

PERMANENT
IMPROVEMENTS
*to the*
HOME *and* GROUNDS

*Beautifying*
*the Home Grounds*

Southern Pine ~

ELLIS DESIGNS ~LATTICE FENCES
ENTRANCE ARCHES ~~~
SES AND GARDEN FURNITURE

hern Pine Association
ORLEANS, LOUISIANA

Improving one's home and beautifying its surroundings were key concepts conveyed in both word and picture in many catalogues in the 1920s and 1930s. Smaller homes, often bungalows or Colonial cottages, appealed to a wide audience. Many were depicted with distinctive red roofs.

12

13

We use this illustration to give you an idea of the thousands of people North, South, East and West who are availing themselves of our offer of Plants and Trees by mail.

# TREES AND PLANTS BY MAIL, POSTPAID.

**At Indian Hill Farm.**

4½ MILES FROM NEWBURYPORT.

☞ As the number of visitors to the Garden and Nursery were so numerous the last season as to occupy more time than could well be spared to their attention, the subscriber has determined to admit no one after 1st June without a ticket, the price of which will be 12½ cents, children half price. The amount will in all cases be returned to those making purchases.

JOHN KYLE, Gardener.

☞ No admittance to the garden on Sundays.

Tickets of admission can now be had at E. Stedman's bookstore, Newburyport, and at the Garden.

One half the proceeds is a perquisite to the Gardener—the other half will be given to some charitable institution.　　June 9

16

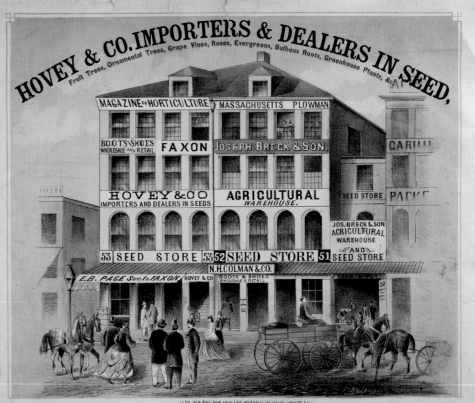

17

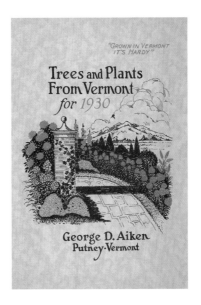

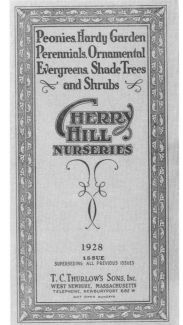

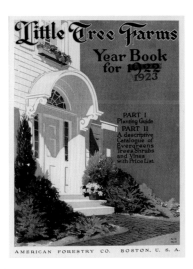

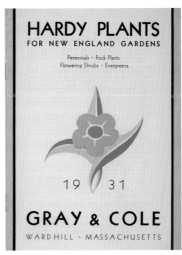

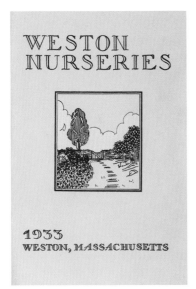

Gardeners rely on skilled plantsmen to provide sturdy and reliable stock at the peak of the spring season for both food production and landscape needs. The earliest nurseries in Massachusetts were established by horticulturalists like Joseph Breck or by former gardeners of large estates. Their offerings included plants and trees as well as seeds.

## Seeds for the Children's Gardens,—
### In Smaller Special Packets at Two Cents per Packet.

No order can be filled for less than **25 cts. for twelve packets,** but this will include copy of the unique New Book, "Small Gardens for Small Folks."

Purchasers, whether children themselves, their parents or teachers, may select any **fifteen varieties for 30 cts.; any twenty for 40 cts., any twenty-five packets for 50 cts.; any fifty packets for $1.00; or $2.00 per one hundred packets,**—assorted as desired.

The price of two cents per packet is **net** and not subject to any discount. We shall be pleased, however, to quote special prices by the thousand packets to teachers and institutions who will pay cost of transportation. With each order of twelve packets for 25 cts., or for fifteen packets or more, at two cents each, we shall give a copy of the little book, "Small Gardens for Small Folks" (price 5 cts.) as advertised on page 168 of The Burpee-Annual for 1913. We shall include also, *if requested,* a free copy of this Bright New Book with *every fifteen packets* of these seeds ordered,—at the rate of two cents per packet.

| No. of pkts. | 30 Annual Flowers. | No. of pkts. | 30 Choice Vegetables. |
|---|---|---|---|
| | 1524 Alyssum, Little Gem. | | 10 Bean, Stringless Green-Pod.★ |
| | 1588 Aster, Semple's Branching, Mixed.★ | | 65 Bean, Fordhook Bush Lima. |
| | 1759 Balsam, Burpee's Defiance, Mixed. | | 117 Beet, Burpee's Columbia.★ |
| | 1809 Calliopsis, Drummondii. | | 137 Beet, Swiss Chard,—Lucullus. |
| | 1864 Celosia, Burpee's Magnificent. | | 176 Cabbage, Enkhuizen Glory. |
| | 1876 Centaurea Imperialis.★ | | 223 Carrot, Burpee's Oxheart.★ |
| | 1884 Centaurea Cyanus (*Cornflower*). | | 301 Corn, Sweet, Golden Bantam.★ |
| | 1935 Cosmos, Early-flowering, Mixed. | | 300 Corn, Pop, Golden Tom Thumb. |
| | 2032 Dianthus, Fordhook Favorites.★ | | 383 Cucumber, Fordhook White Spine. |
| | 2049 Eschscholtzia, Golden West. | | 476 Lettuce, Earliest Wayahead. |
| | 2086 Gaillardia, Picta Lorenziana. | | 530 Lettuce, Burpee's Iceberg.★ |
| | 2118 Kochia Tricophylla (*Burning Bush*).★ | | 544 Musk Melon, Burpee's Netted Gem, or "Rocky Ford."★ |
| | 2124 Larkspur, Tall Rocket, Mixed. | | 574 Musk Melon, Burpee's Fordhook. |
| | 2178 Marigold, Orange Ball. | | 588 Watermelon, Fordhook Early. |
| | 2232 Mignonette, Fordhook Finest, Mixed.★ | | 647 Mustard, Fordhook Fancy.★ |
| | 2354 Nasturtium, Gorgeous Tom Thumb. | | 666 Okra, Kleckley's Favorite. |
| | 2476 Pansy, Imperial German, Mixed.★ | | 681 Onion, Prize-Taker.★ |
| | 2556 Petunia, Enchantress.★ | | 687 Onion, Red Wethersfield. |
| | 2581 Phlox Drummondii, Fordhook Large-Flowering, Mixed.★ | | 717 Parsley, Extra Curled Dwarf.★ |
| | 2636 Poppy, Fordhook Fairies. | | 737 Peas, Prolific Extra-Early. |
| | 2707 Scabiosa, Large Double, Mixed. | | 753 Peas, Little Marvel. |
| | 2756 Sunflower, Stella.★ | | 818 Pepper, Neapolitan. |
| | 2780 Verbena Hybrida, Extra Fine, Mixed. | | 861 Pumpkin, Small Sugar. |
| | 2813 Zinnia, Mammoth Tall, Mixed. | | 878 Radish, Burpee's Rapid-Red. |
| | 2911 Canary-Bird Flower. | | 938 Radish, White Icicle.★ |
| | 2923 Cypress Vine, Mixed. | | 1008 Spinach, New Zealand. |
| | 3021 Morning Glory, Tall Mixed.★ | | 1032 Squash, Burpee's Fordhook. |
| | 3060 Nasturtium, Tall Variegated Queen, Mixed.★ | | 1101 Tomato, Chalk's Early Jewel.★ |
| | 3371 Sweet Pea, Best Mixed Grandiflora. | | 1095 Tomato, Burpee's Dwarf-Giant. |
| | 3599 Sweet Pea, Burpee's Surpassingly Superb Spencers for 1913, Mixed.★ | | 1157 Turnip, Purple-Top Strap-Leaf.★ |

★ The **Twelve Flowers** marked with a star (★), together with a copy of the bright new book— Small Gardens for Small Folks,—will be mailed for **25 cts.** ☞ You can select, of course, any twelve packets (with book) for 25 cts. ☞ Five of these "*Ready-Made*" *Collections* (each with the book) will be mailed for $1.00.

★ The **Twelve Vegetables** marked with star (★), together with a copy of the bright new book— Small Gardens for Small Folks,—will be mailed **for 25 cts.,** or Five Collections for $1.00, and mailed to five separate addresses if so directed. ☞ You may make *your own selection,* of course, of any twelve packets,—with the book,—for 25 cts.

You can use this circular as an **order sheet,**— and extra copies will be sent upon application.

W. ATLEE BURPEE & CO., Philadelphia.

Date,_____1913.

For enclosed remittance of_____you will please forward promptly, postpaid, the following *Seeds for the Children's Gardens.*

| Numbers ordered | | |
|---|---|---|
| | Separate Packets as marked above at **2 cts. each** . . . . . . . . . . . | $ |
| | Ready-Made Collection of Twelve Flowers, *as starred* (★), with The Book . . . . . | |
| | Ready-Made Collection of Twelve Vegetables, *as starred* (★), with The Book . . . | |
| | Burpee's **Combination-Collection** of Seeds for the Children's Gardens, seven Flowers and five Vegetables, with The Book, *as advertised on the other side* . . | |
| | TOTAL . . . . . . . . . . . | |

You will forward with the seeds_____copies of "Small Gardens for Small Folks," to which I am entitled,

Name,_____
(Ladies will please put the prefix **Miss** or **Mrs.**)

Street Address or Box Number_____

Post Office,_____

County,_____

R. D. Route,_____State,_____

☞ Please check (✓) here if you desire (either for yourself or a friend) BURPEE'S ANNUAL FOR 1913.—**as advertised on the other side.**

---

Designs of seed packets progressed from those with a simple bordered imprint of the seed name as produced by the Shakers to ones with colorful representations of flowers and vegetables that were boxed for display in grocery, hardware, and general stores. Many companies packaged seeds of easily grown plants to introduce children to gardening.

Peter Henderson's fiftieth anniversary catalogue provided its readers with images of all aspects of its extensive operation, including the staff artist drawing pictures of flowers to use in catalogues. In the early decades of the twentieth century, D. M. Ferry and Company of Detroit commissioned well-known artist Maxfield Parrish to create nursery rhyme-themed pictures for its advertisements and seed packets.

**Mary Mary quite contrary
How does your garden grow?
PLANT**

**FERRY'S SEEDS**

**Seed Order for CHAS. C. HART SEED CO.**

1923    WETHERSFIELD, CONN.    1923

Date_____    Enclosed find following amount:
Name_____    P. O. Money Order_____
Post Office_____    Express Money Order_____
Express Office_____    Draft_____
Freight Station_____    Check_____
                            Cash_____
            R. F. D. No._____    Stamps_____

E WHETHER WANTED BY MAIL, EXPRESS OR FREIGHT

| NAMES OF SEEDS WANTED | Price | Amount |
|---|---|---|
|  |  |  |
|  |  |  |
|  |  |  |
|  |  |  |
|  |  |  |
|  |  |  |
|  |  |  |
|  |  |  |
|  |  |  |

36

LIVINGSTON'S SEED ANNUAL 1903.

LIVINGSTON'S TRUE BLUE SEEDS

VEGETABLES

1923 PLANT HARTS SEEDS

CHAS. C. HART SEED CO. CONN.

Seed companies were continually improving varieties of vegetables, which they then featured prominently in their catalogues. Then as now order forms were an integral part of the catalogue. A self-addressed envelope was often included for ease in ordering.

34

37

40

Chromolithography revolutionized the appearance of seed catalogues in the 1890s. Vibrantly colored depictions of mouth-watering fruits or exquisitely detailed flowers filled their pages, greatly enhancing their appeal to potential purchasers.

1 GOLDEN QUEEN
2 CUTHBERT

3 MUSKINGUM.
4 EARHART.

## FOUR BEST RASPBERRIES.

LITHO. BY H. M. WALL, BROOKLYN, N.Y.

41

43

44

45

Summer roses are both romantic and symbolic, and perhaps are the most cherished (and some would say fussy) plants for the garden. Bulbs announce spring and the beginning of the gardening season. Beatrice Stevens's enchanting illustration of the young woman gazing at the sundial is in the style of Kate Greenaway.

47

46

HOTCHKISS
INSECT POWDER DISTRIBUTOR.

THE CURRIE FERTILIZER CO.,
LOUISVILLE, KY.

FIRST PRIZE POTATO

The Return from the Insect Fair.

[over]

48

Many products in the 1880s were promoted using the artistic conventions of the day as well as a bit of humor. Several companies used the same anthropomorphic vegetables on both trade cards and seed packets, including the Jerome B. Rice Company of Cambridge, New York (see page 46).

51

52

# Everything for the Garden

### NINETEEN HUNDRED EIGHTEEN

## Peter Henderson & Co.

### 35 & 37 CORTLANDT ST. · NEW YORK

MOUNT VERNON, VA. THE HOME OF GEORGE WASHINGTON
—See Page 2

# EVERYTHING
## *for the* GARDEN
### 1932
# PETER HENDERSON & CO.
## 35 CORTLANDT ST., NEW YORK

55

Colonial Arm Chair

PATENTED

Garland pattern. A period design pleasingly interpreted.

No. 540 S   Standard Size...................$25.00
No. 540½ S   Large Size ...................... 40.00

2

Colonial Table

Garland pattern. A beautiful expression of the revived interest in things Colonial.

No. 544 S   Diameter 30 inches (four legs).....$45.00
No. 545 S   Diameter 25 inches (three legs)....  36.00

6

56

EVERYTHING FOR THE GARDEN
1933
PETER HENDERSON & CO
35 CORTLANDT ST.
NEW YORK

Copyright 1933 by Peter Henderson & Co., New York, N.Y.

ASH LAWN, VA. THE HOME OF PRESIDENT MONROE    See Page 81

57

Beginning in the late nineteenth century, America's past became an inspiration for architects, furniture designers, and even gardeners. These covers depict romantic representations of historic houses in Virginia, including the one for Mount Vernon, which honors the bicentennial of George Washington's birth in 1932. The "Colonial Arm Chair" is in fact a variation of a neoclassical garden chair designed in 1835 by Prussian architect Karl Friedrich Schinkel.

List of Parts and Directions for Use of

# THE=GREAT=AMERICAN

## BALL BEARING===LAWN MOWER

Lists of Parts of Great American Ball Bearing Lawn Mower
15, 17, 19 and 21 Inches.

### DIAGRAM OF PARTS

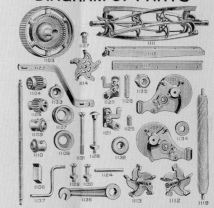

**Order The Great American Ball Bearing Lawn Mower**

### TO ADJUST THE LOWER KNIFE.

*After* adjusting the revolving cutter, adjust the lower knife by loosening the two top screws which bear on the end of the lower knife, both alike, and tightening the two lower screws.

This adjusting process should be kept up until the lower knife *barely* touches the revolving cutter from end to end, without binding.

Be sure that all the screws are tightened before using the Mower.

eft hand

ich runs

left end;

rning the

n top of

n the re-

with the

sting the

# EXCELSIOR SIDE WHEEL MOWER.

MANUFACTURED BY

**Chadborn & Coldwell Mfg.**
NEWBURG

The lawn mower was invented in England by Edwin Budding in 1830. American improvements created more lightweight machines that were successfully mass-produced. They were so lightweight that women and children were featured pushing them in many early trade cards. Today the riding mower is the mower of choice and we no longer dress up to mow the lawn.

"NEW CHAMPION FORCE PUMP"
✢ CLARK BROS. BELMONT, N.Y.

Also Manufacturers of Clarks Improved.
✢ Ratchet Stocks & Pipe Vises.

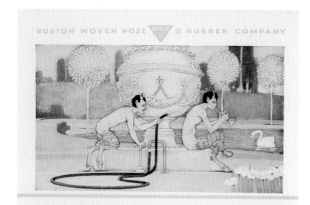

BOSTON WOVEN HOSE & RUBBER COMPANY

## GARDEN HOSE

ALF a century ago gardens were watered from pails and sprinkling pots—a slow and laborious method. The only hose known was that of riveted leather, 2½ inches in diameter, which was being used by the Fire Departments.

¶ There were some improvements in the construction of hand-made hose, but the most important progress was made when the first hose machine was brought to this country from England in 1865.

¶ Until 1892 all garden hose was made with a rubber tube, three plies of canvas, and a cover. In that year we introduced the multiple construction—using several plies of fine, closely woven duck, instead of only three plies. This method of construction produced a hose of much greater strength than could be obtained in any other way.

4

64

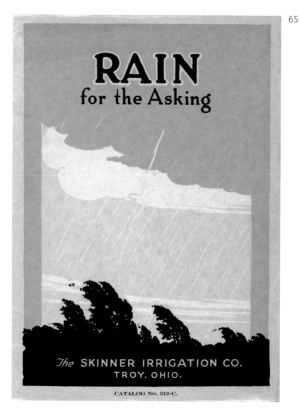

# RAIN
## for the Asking

The SKINNER IRRIGATION CO.
TROY, OHIO.

CATALOG No. 313-C.

Water is essential for garden plants to flourish. A simple watering can can be sufficient for a small plot but hoses, sprinklers, and irrigation systems are necessities for larger gardens, especially vegetable gardens. The Boston Woven Hose and Rubber Company issued a catalogue that provided historical background on the product it manufactured (64). Many early seed catalogues featured pages of garden tools and other accessories.

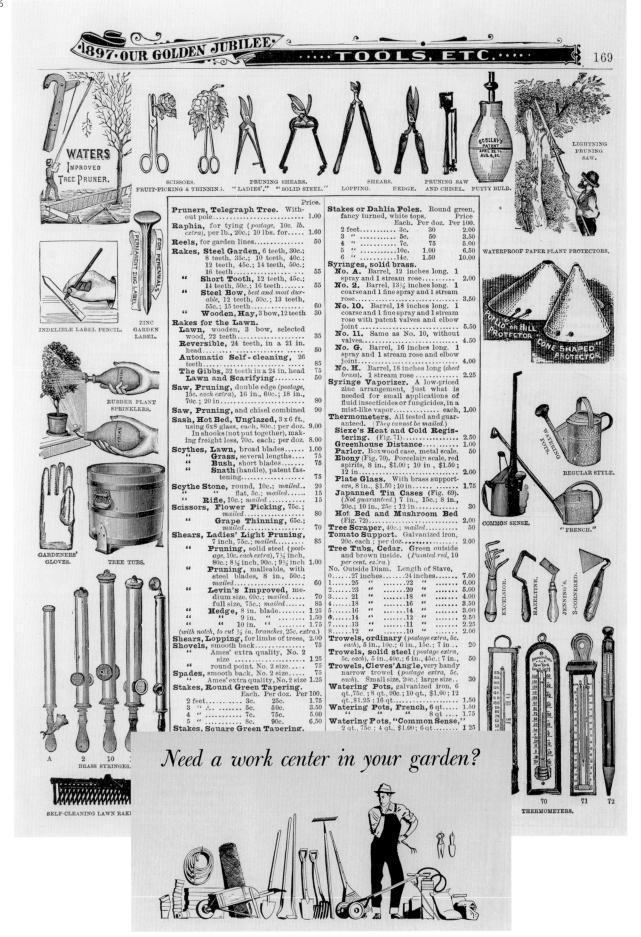

*Need a work center in your garden?*

# THE OUTDOOR LIVING ROOM FOR 1935 . . .

In all the gliders, chairs and umbrellas, we have arranged a number of matching or harmonizing groups and for the pieces not shown on pages 4-7 and 35-37 we invite your inquiry addressed to the Metal Furniture Department.

Prices of items shown here may be found on pages 4, 5, 7 and 36.

As Americans moved to the suburbs, they also moved many activities outdoors. The backyard was no longer only for the garden but was divided into areas for play and relaxation. Barbequing became popular; today, entire kitchens are incorporated into backyard patios.

68

OVERLOOK

FOUNTAIN GATE

OUTDOOR LIVING ROOM

HOUSE

## THE LIMITED AREA ROOM PATIO TYPE

IN CERTAIN types of homes, especially in California and the South, the architecture requires a patio type of outdoor living room. This plan, like the one preceding, is designed for a small area, yet may be enlarged, in proportion, for larger space. Beds along the walls and each side of the center space provide ample area for characteristic plants and flowers.

PORCH

HOUSE

HOW TO MAKE AN OUTDOOR LIVING ROOM

PRICE 25 CENTS

J. W. ADAMS NURSERY COMPANY
POST OFFICE, SPRINGFIELD, MASS.
NURSERY, WESTFIELD, MASS.

71

**Walpole**

**Cedar Furniture**

70

## Q. P. WOVEN HAMMOCKS.

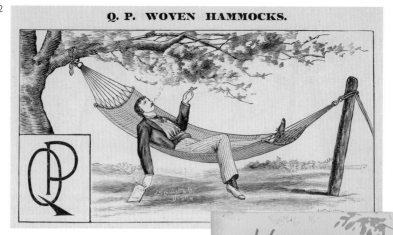

72

73

### Arvin
NATIONALLY ADVERTISED

## METAL OUTDOOR FURNITURE

STYLE 10 CHAIR

Distinctive
styling...

Outstanding
value!

STYLE 20 ROCKER

STYLE 500 TABLE

**CHECK THESE FEATURES:**
Raymond Loewy decorator colors. Selected by famous Raymond Loewy Associates for fresh new interest and individuality.
Perforated seats and backs. For added beauty, resiliency; for ventilation and quick drainage.
Flared arm rests. Added width where needed most makes both chair and rocker roomier.
Sturdy, long-life construction. Extra strong tubular steel frame; easy-to-assemble snug-fit joints give continuous stream-lined frame effect; comfort-contour perforated seats and backs of 20-gauge shaped steel with deep turned rolled edges.
Rust and weather resistant. Electronically sprayed baked enamel finish over Bonderized metal is extra durable, cleans easily, keeps lustre.
Handy grip carton. Convenient fold-back flap for easy cash-and-carry portability.
America's No. 1 value. Promotionally priced for quick turnover. Leading traffic-builders in the outdoor furniture field.

Manufactured by **ARVIN INDUSTRIES, Inc.,** Columbus, Indiana • Metal Chrome-Plated Dinette Sets • All-Metal Ironing Tables • Outdoor furniture
Nationally Distributed by *Salmanson & Co., Inc.* 1107 BROADWAY, NEW YORK 10, N. Y.   American Furniture Mart, Chicago 11 Western Merchandise Mart, San Francisco 3

*Hampden Outdoor Furniture*

HAMPDEN OUTDOOR FURNITURE

74

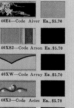

No. 40E4
Pat. No. 1676074
Pat. No. 1767736

No. 240S
Pat. No. 1676074
Pat. No. 1767736

| Frame | Cover | | Cover | | Frame |
|---|---|---|---|---|---|
| | No. 40—Code Arbor Ea.....$4.30 | | No. 40EW—Code Apron Ea..$5.70 | | |
| | No. 40LS2—Code Aillt Ea..$5.70 | | No. 40E3—Code Agaze Ea..$5.70 | | |
| | No. 40GS2—Code Amend Ea.$5.70 | | No. 40E4—Code Aiver Ea..$5.70 | | |
| | No. 40GW—Code Alarm Ea. $5.70 | | No. 40XS2—Code Arson Ea..$5.70 | | |
| | No. 40G3—Code Acana Ea..$5.70 | | No. 40XW—Code Array Ea..$5.70 | | |
| | No. 40G4—Code Alaja Ea..$5.70 | | No. 40X3—Code Acies Ea..$5.70 | | |
| | No. 40ES2—Code Aorta Ea..$5.70 | | No. 40X4—Code Airus Ea..$5.70 | | |

Color Swatch No. 4

75

New types of furniture and fabrics were developed for use outdoors. Lighter aluminum furniture was more informal looking and more easily moved than cast iron or heavy wooden tables, chairs, and benches. Brightly colored, more weather-resistant canvas, oil cloth, and plastic covered chairs and lounges.

**METALART**

**OUTDOOR CHAIRS**

*of Recognized*

*Leadership*

**METALART COMPANY** INC.

**PATERSON – NEW JERSEY**

78

## Ready-Made Gardens for Sun or Shade

Our preplanned gardens are all designed using reliable, carefree plants that will grow splendidly and look marvelous for many years to come. Each is accompanied by an easy-to-follow planting plan. These gardens are a convenience for experienced gardeners, and a terrific way for novices to make a successful start. Plants are shipped in 1 pint pots, 2 qt pots, or bareroot.

**To view more gardens plus details about each collection, visit whiteflowerfarm.com/preplannedgardens**

**MONARCH BUTTERFLY GARDEN**
Enjoy the beauty of Monarch butterflies while joining efforts to help support them with our colorful Monarch Butterfly Garden. It includes 2 varieties of Milkweed, the essential (and only) food Monarch caterpillars eat, plus other favorite plants such as Liatris, Coneflower, Salvia, and Joe Pye Weed. These host and nectar-rich plants will help sustain Monarchs through all their life stages. Includes 15 plants and covers about 48 sq ft.

Z4–7S/9W MAY–SEP HT60"
**S83193** *each collection $135, 2 for $131 each*

**MONARCH BUTTERFLY GARDEN**

**30 | PREPLANNED GARDENS**

SMALL SPACE SHADE GARDEN

77

79

## Blue Ribbon Garden Essentials
Watering Wand S7732 *$39* | Hose S7737 *$59* |
Hats S55145, S55144, S55143 *$49 each* | Gloves S55
Garden Tote S57109 *$99* | Brush S50709 *$15* | C
**64 | ACCESSORIES**      Visit whiteflowerfarm

WETHERSFIELD SEED GARDENS · SINCE 1811
200 Years **COMSTOCK SEEDS** 2011 Catalog
COMSTOCK, FERRE & CO. LLC.      WETHERSFIELD, CONN.

*Since 1818* **BRECK'S**

**DAVID AUSTIN®**

80

81

82

*ndbook of Roses 2010*
ELEVENTH USA EDITION

Garden catalogues today truly do offer everything for the garden—
even tailor-made "preplanned gardens" and "garden essentials"
like those available from Connecticut's White Flower Farm (77, 79).
Companies like Comstock Ferre and Breck's have celebrated 200
years of providing seed to the nation's gardeners. Heirloom seeds
and organic methods now have great appeal. And David Austin has
brought back the scent that had been bred out of many roses.

1

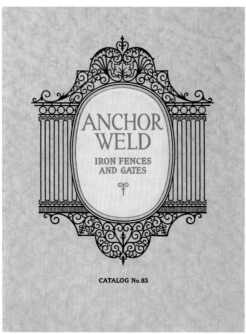

2

3

# BEYOND THE GARDEN GATE

## ART, ARCHITECTURE, AND ORNAMENT

Richard C. Nylander

One of the pleasures of visiting gardens on local tours or at historic houses and grand estates open to the public is being inspired by the endless variety of plans, plantings, and decorative features that professional or amateur designers have incorporated into the whole scheme. While some of us are content looking only for the name of a particular flower or vine, others observe more closely the manipulation of space, the sense of scale, and details. The last includes the pattern of planting areas, paving materials, straight and wandering paths, focal points, and the selection of defining architectural and decorative features—the bones that will remain after the flowers have gone by.

Each component of a garden has a purpose, most of them practical, some whimsical. Garden gates invite us in. Fences and walls create boundaries and protect the plantings. Paths and steps lead us on to investigate different areas or perhaps to a surprise or a dead end. Urns and statues provide focal points and treillage lends an air of sophistication. Structures like summer houses allow us to sit down and enjoy the view. Ordinary sheds are necessary to store our tools and pots while today's decorated she-sheds offer a space to express a personality and savor privacy.

In addition to the books noted in chapter one, there was a whole category of publications in the early twentieth century that focused solely on decorative accessories that could enhance a basic garden layout. At that time, the terms garden architecture, garden ornament, and garden furniture were all-encompassing and used interchangeably to describe the same features. The tables of contents in these books—and in fact in books on the same subjects today—are remarkably similar, with chapters devoted to summer houses, pergolas, arbors, paths, garden steps, sundials, pools, and fountains, to name a few. The texts range from romantic histories of a particular form to lengthy descriptions of what each author thought were the correct proportions and materials.

Well-illustrated articles in periodicals during this time also focused on these same features and how they could be used in an urban courtyard, a suburban garden, or a larger country home or estate. Words in the captions like "successful," "practical," "well-placed," and "simple and attractive" emphasized the effectiveness of what was pictured. While books and articles told the reader how certain features fit into the whole garden scheme, catalogues offered an endless variety from which to choose. And therein, according to more than one author, lay the "great opportunity for the display of good and poor taste." Suitability is a key point stressed in all these publications. The style of the garden, its architectural features, and its ornament should be compatible with its surrounding environment and the architecture of the house. An ornate garden with cast iron urns and fountains designed for a high-style Victorian mansion would not be appropriate next to a streamlined Modern dwelling, nor would a summer house in the form of a classical temple in the cottage garden of a Cape Cod house.

While many garden features could be made by a carpenter (and there were numerous manuals for the handyman), several ready-made types were available for purchase, most commonly arbors and trellises. Arbors took on a variety of forms, from the simple arch at the entrance to a suburban garden to larger structures enclosing benches and perhaps a table and serving more as a summer house. Complicated schemes echoing elaborate European treillage constructs were available "complete with working drawings and photographs." Simple lattice panels were more common, having always been extremely useful in the garden to support plantings, but also to divide different areas and hide utilitarian spaces. Henrietta C. Peabody in *Outside the House Beautiful* (1923) warns, however, "the only danger is using it [latticework] too freely that it becomes tiresome."

Guy Lowell, in *American Gardens* (1902), states that "the arbor, the pergola, and the summer house have always been the principal ornamental architectural features of the garden." Indeed, summer houses have graced the New England landscape since the eighteenth century and range from those with Georgian and neoclassical detail to latticed Gothic fantasies. Pergolas became fashionable with the popularity of the Italian garden in the late nineteenth century and were an integral part of many Colonial Revival gardens of the same period.

Several books on garden architecture and ornament note that "garden beauty and harmony need not necessitate lavish expenditure." Indeed, catalogues provided products for every economic level and taste. The W. A. Snow Company of Boston illustrated offerings from the highly ornamental wrought iron entrance gates custom-made for industrial magnate Henry Clay Frick to utilitarian "unclimb-able chainlink" used for fencing in both public parks and private backyards.

By the early twentieth century greenhouses were no longer only for the wealthy. Greenhouse manufacturers offered a range of structures for grand estates, for homeowners, and for nurserymen, varying in size from a lean-to to "out of the ordinary installations." The catalogue for the American Greenhouse Manufacturing Company declares "a greenhouse is a necessary part of a well-planned garden" and states definitively that "no matter where you live, if you have a house and lawn, you should have a greenhouse." Not only were they useful for starting seedlings and over-wintering plants but they were also promoted as being beneficial to the owner's health, providing a wholesome hobby, and even aiding with a tan! "Health giving, joy bringing," exclaimed one Lord and Burnham catalogue.

Concrete is one of the most versatile materials for garden features, long used for walls and pools and molded into edging, benches, urns, and planters. Many of these items were available commercially but books like *Concrete Pottery and Garden Furniture* by Ralph C. Davison (1910) also gave the "amateur craftsman" detailed instructions on "how to turn concrete into objects of art" for the garden. One could even turn concrete into a profitable personal business, as promoted by the Michigan company Colorcrete Industries in its colorfully illustrated catalogue *Colorcrete: The New Gateway to Money-making Opportunities.*

Some kind of statue or other sculpture may be what first comes to most people's minds when the term garden ornament is mentioned. An enormous range has always been available from reproductions of antique statuary to figures from popular culture, such as Sylvia Shaw Judson's *Bird Girl* of 1936, made famous on the cover of the 1994 book *Midnight in the Garden of Good and Evil*. Garden gnomes, found as early as the 1840s in English gardens, the ever-popular Saint Francis, and the pink flamingo created by Don Featherstone in Leominster, Massachusetts, in 1957 never seem to go out of style. Surprisingly, life-like representations of real-life garden pests such as rabbits and squirrels are widely available and oddly welcomed into many gardens in their inanimate form. Urns and decorative terra cotta flowerpots also abound. With so much choice, discipline is needed both in the selection and placement of ornaments so that the garden does not become a jungle of incongruous forms. Many garden writers suggest that if one has room for only one ornament in the garden, it should be a sundial on a pedestal.

In his 1906 book *The Garden and Its Accessories* landscape architect Loring Underwood wrote that "the designing of gardens and the selection of their accessories is as much an art as painting." Like a painting, a garden can be abstract, impressionistic, or rich in period detail. While much depends on plantings, the choices made for a garden's architectural features and decorative ornaments contribute greatly to its overall success.

4

5

6

7

In the late nineteenth century, pergolas became a popular feature in both extensive formal gardens of large estates and their more intimate "old-fashioned" counterparts designed to complement Colonial houses. The structure came by way of Italy, where its original purpose was to support grape vines. Later, any flowering vine was appropriate to add color and some shade.

8

9

TRELLIS FOR E.L.WINTHROP ESQ
NEWPORT R.I.

SCALE ¾=1'-0"

OGDEN CODMAN ARCH'T
WINDOOR ARCADE NEW YORK

10

11

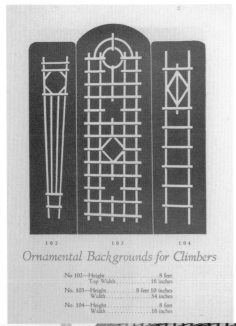

No 102    103    104
*Ornamental Backgrounds for Climbers*

No. 102—Height...................8 feet
          Top Width............16 inches
No. 103—Height.........8 feet 10 inches
          Width.................34 inches
No. 104—Height...................8 feet
          Width.................16 inches

The Joy of Living
*Out of Doors*

13

To support climbing plants, trellis and latticework could be used by themselves as a simple frame, attached to an arbor, or incorporated within an elaborate primary architectural garden feature. Numerous variations were either architect-designed, purchased ready-made, or constructed by a carpenter or homeowner from plans in magazines or mail-order kits.

16

17

18

Summer houses are places for shelter, repose, or play. In times past, their style often echoed that of the principal structure on the property. Sometimes, however, they exhibited a different and more fanciful architectural treatment. Whatever their style, they become a focal point in the garden.

19

ERIES, AMERICAN VIEWS.

20

"In a greenhouse it is always summer" was the enticing phrase coined by one manufacturer of glass houses. One of the oldest surviving greenhouses in New England was built by wealthy merchant Theodore Lyman in the early nineteenth century (23, and page 105). A century later, greenhouses were being promoted as within the reach of most homeowners.

21

Glass enclosures

22

LORD & BURNHAM CO
G R E E N H O U S E
DESIGNERS AND
MANUFACTURERS

J. W. & J. S. MOULTON, SALEM, MASS.

23

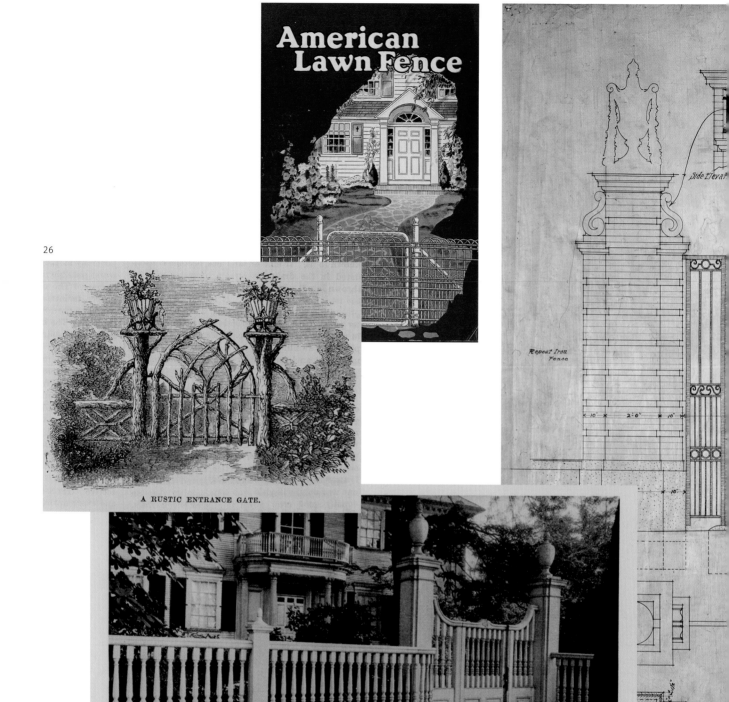

24

25

26

A RUSTIC ENTRANCE GATE.

*Old Portsmouth furnishes this classic example of architectural harmony between house and fence. Note the perfect proportions of the gateway.*

27

Fences and gateways often anticipate the style of the dwelling or the spirit of the garden that lies beyond. One assumes that the gates depicted in the architectural drawing (25) lead to a grand house via a long drive and that the rustic gate opens into a small cottage garden. A Colonial Revival fence harmonizes with the eighteenth-century Governor John Langdon House in Portsmouth, New Hampshire (27), while the chain-link fence is more practical than beautiful (24).

- INCH SCALE DRAWING OF FORE
- COVRT FENCE AND GATES FROM
- MAIN AVENVE · HOVSE FOR ·
- A C FRICK ESQ AT PRIDES MASS

- Little & Browne Architects -
- 70 Kilby St Boston Mass -
- February 6, 1905      (C.F.K. & T.W.M.)

(61)

Revised Sept. 23, '05
C.C.H.

Note that in the revision a basket is shown on this post

-NOTE- Urns to be modelled and Submitted to Architects for approval

Basket Ornament on Posts (see ¼ Scale Plan)

~ Elevation of Gate and Fence ~

~ Section through Granite Base ~

ANCHOR · POST · IRON · WORKS

28

## 33

29

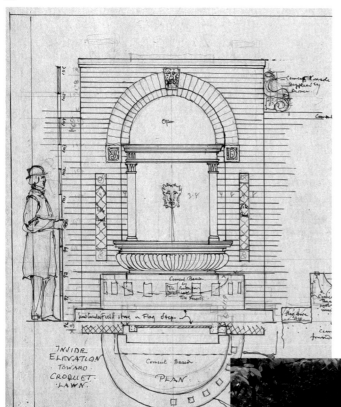

30

31

No. 399  Fountain
35 in. h. to rim, 37 in. w., 24⅜ in. b., $100.00
No. 710 Figure, $35.00 additional
Combined height, 61 in.

32

Water creates additional interest in any garden. Whether it cascades from a fountain, flows from an impressive architectural folly, or drips from the walls of a secluded grotto, it pleases the ear as well as the eye.

## 34

### GALLOWAY POTTERY

#### Bird Baths

A bird bath in your garden is an invitation to the birds to tarry with you and enliven the scene with their merry notes, while at the same time rendering you much practical service. It is a true gloom dispeller, as well as being essential to the welfare of the garden. A garden is incomplete without one.

**BIRD BATH**
No. 442
Also made in turquoise glaze, $50.00

No. 650
37 in. h., 24 in. w.
15 in. b., $32.50

No. 699
Same with bowl 30 in. w.
$45.00

No. 654
35 in. h., 25 in. w.
12 in. b., $28.50

No. 653
Same without festoon
$27.50

No. 441
34 in. h., 25 in. w.
13 in. b., $30.00

No. 442
34 in. h., 23 in. w.
13 in. b., $25.00

COLOR: Bird Baths are carried in stock in the high-fired light stony-gray, unless otherwise mentioned.

10

Attracting birds to a garden has many advantages in controlling pests as long as they don't become pests themselves. Birdhouses come in many shapes and sizes, the simplest often built as projects or gifts by enterprising children. Birdbaths, like sundials, can become the focal point of a small garden.

36

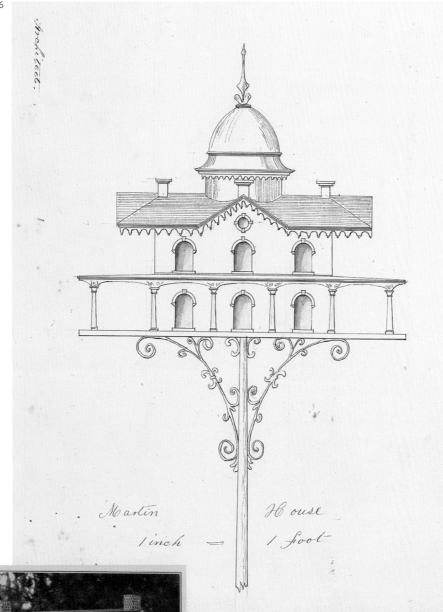

Martin House

1 inch = 1 foot

*Dutch Colonial Bird House*
*24 x 40 inches—32 rooms—16 ft. Pole—Price $36.00*
*Without Pole, $30.03*

37

Fig. 5. Exhibit of Birdhouses Made in the St. Johnsbury Schools in 1919.

38

## 39

## VASES AND CONTAINERS

Our carefully selected stock of plant containers, pots and vases is large and varied. We carry goods of both domestic and foreign manufacture, including everything from plain clay pots to the richly finished glazed terra cotta vases. A few interesting pieces are listed here. In addition to these we have at our glass garden store many other attractive and useful articles for the garden and outdoor living room.

*Terra Cotta Pot No. 600*

*Fluted Pot No. 61*

*Antique Box No. 539*

*Rustic Box LZ*

*Pot and Saucer No. 541*

**Fluted Vase No. 61**
An unusually attractive design made unglazed in red or brown terra cotta, and glazed in yellow, jade or blue. Height 11½ inches, base 7 inches, opening 11½ inches, unglazed $4.00; glazed $8.00. Height 19½ inches, 11 inch base, opening 19½ inches, unglazed $11.00, glazed $20.00, f. o. b. California.

**Antique Box No. 539**
Gray artificial stone. Simple effective design. Height 10 inches, top 14 inches, $4.00. Express collect.

**Rustic Box LZ**
Made of gray artificial stone. For indoor or outdoor use. 10½ inches square, 8 inches deep. $3.00. Express collect.

**Pot and Saucer No. 541**
Attractive Italian design in gray stone with medallions on the sides, 13 inch top diameter. $4.00. Express collect.

**Sunchaser No. 1**
Very new! For particular people! A revolving plant stand that allows large potted plants to be turned easily so that all parts may grow toward the light. Made of heavy copper, mounted on ball bearings. Can be used as a stand, 6 inch base, or reversed as a water-tight revolving saucer to hold 9 inch pot. Will not rust. $3.75. Express collect.

**Flower Vase No. 37**
A graceful pottery vase in green, rose, blue, lavender or yellow. For tall flowers or a lamp base. $2.00. Express collect.

**Tall Garden Vase No. 337**
A gracefully designed garden or terrace jar in unglazed clay, light and dark brown shades. 19¾ inches high. $5.00 each. Express collect.

**Terra Cotta Pot No. 600**
Fill with evergreens for indoor or outdoor use. Light gray, red, pink, caen stone and buff. 13 inches high, 18½ inches wide, 9½ inch base. $8.00.
No. 600½. 14 inches high, 20½ inches wide, 10½ inch base. $10.75.
No. 601. 16 inches high, 23 inches wide, 12 inch base. $15.00.
Express or freight collect.

**Pot No. 513**

**Terra Cotta Pot No. 49**
Very inexpensive. Splendid for garden or terrace. 9½ inches high, 13 inches wide, 6 inch base. $2.50.

**Terra Cotta Pot No. 51**
Same as No. 49. 11 inches high, 17 inches wide, 9 inch base. $6.25.
No. 52. 12 inches high. 21 inches wide, 11 inch base. $9.50.
No. 53. 15 inches high. 24 inches wide, 14 inch base. $14.50. Express or freight collect.

**Lion Box No. 34**
Gray artificial stone, 8 inches high, 8 inches wide. Price $2.00. Express collect.

**Hanging Gypsy Kettle No. 843**
New. Splendid for hanging plants indoors or out of doors. Natural iron finish, with inside container. Complete $6.00. Express collect.

**Strawberry Jar and Stand No. 394**
A delightful, unglazed clay finished jar, fitted into a very graceful, hand wrought iron stand. An artistic addition to the increasingly popular ivy stand. Height 12½ inches. $5.00 complete. Strawberry Jar alone, $1.50. Express collect.

**Indian Bowl No. 38**
Of unglazed terra cotta, made by expert native craftsmen. Colors brown and red. Width 18 inches. $7.50 f. o. b. California. Illustrated center below.

**Garden Vase No. 111**
Exquisite. Beautifully glazed terra cotta. Choice of 6 colors.* Height 27 inches, top width 12 inches. $55.00 f. o. b. California. Illustrated center below.

**Vase No. 105**
Interesting vase for indoors or outdoors. Glazed terra cotta in blue or yellow. 22½ inches high, $10.00 each. 30 inches high $15.00 f. o. b. California. Illustrated center below.

**Vase No. 118**
Glazed terra cotta. Choice of 6 colors.* Height 18 inches, top width 14½ inches $16.00 each f. o. b. California.

**Palm Pot No. 225**
Attractive glazed terra cotta pots in 6 rich colors.* Height 11½ inches, top width 12 inches. $7.00. Height 17½ inches, top width 18 inches. $11.00. f. o. b. California.

**Vase No. 58**
An interesting low vase in glazed terra cotta, blue or yellow. Height 11 inches, width 16 inches, opening 12 inches. $6.00 f. o. b. California.

*Terra Cotta Pot No. 513*

*Terra Cotta Pot No. 629*

*Terra Cotta Pot No. 49*

*Lion Box No. 34*

*Gypsy Kettle No. 843*

Light gray, 12 inches high, 17 inches . . . . . or freight . . . . . . . . . 12 inches . . . base. $10.00.

. . . bright blue green, pink flushed tan, flesh mottled pink and yellow, . . . light gray with darker flecks.

No. 105    No. 118    No. 225    No. 58
. . . figured design is typical of our Danish ware.

*Strawberry Jar Alone, $1.50*
*With Wrought Iron Stand No. 394 Complete $5.00*

## 40

Vol. IV     SEPTEMBER, 1907     No. 9

Herbert Browne coll.

# AMERICAN·HOMES
## AND
## ~GARDENS~

$3.00 A YEAR     MUNN & COMPANY, Publishers     PRICE, 25 CENTS

43

What would a garden be without pots or urns? They are both practical and ornamental, ranging from basic terra cotta flowerpots to decorative concrete, cast iron, or marble urns. The variety is endless.

# Rich, Textured Color Effects are Obtained Through The Entire Field of COLORCRETE Units. Nothing can approach its enduring charm

To produce charm and beauty, and have it for a permanent source of pleasure and admiration, is the mission of Colorcrete.

*The Moorish Jar*

*The Plymouth*

*The Grecian Urn*

*Landscapes enhanced with Colorcrete*

*The Corinthian*

*The Birdfont*

*Colonial Seat*

*De Luxe Bench*

*Happy Hour Sundial*

46

Fig. 8. Applying the shellac to the clay mold.

45

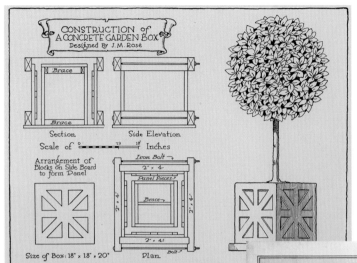

47

HOW TO MAKE
CONCRETE
GARDEN
FURNITURE
*and*
ACCESSORIES

edited by
JOHN T. FALLON

48

COLORCRETE
The
New Gateway
to Money-making
Opportunities

Colorcrete Industries
Holland - Michigan

Books and catalogues promoting the versatility of concrete are filled with information and pictures on how to make every imaginable garden ornament as well as ideas on how to use them around the home.

50

Statues and other figural representations set the tone for the garden. Some are classically inspired while others are totally whimsical. Selection of this type of garden ornament is purely a matter of taste.

53

54

55

## YARD and GARDEN

### TARKINGTON BAKER

56

| No. 474 | No. 295 | No. 476 |
| --- | --- | --- |
| 31 in. h., 11¾ in. t. | 34 in. h., 13 in. t. | 31 in. h., 11¾ in. t. |
| 12 in. b., $18.50 | 12 in. b., $22.50 | 10 in. b., $20.00 |

Much has been written on the history of sundials, the mottos and sentiments engraved on their surfaces, and their placement in the garden. They are a focal point in many gardens, often on axis with other decorative elements.

**Celia Thaxter's Garden**

APPLEDORE ISLAND

*Isles of Shoals, Maine*

# WHERE FLOWERS NEVER FADE

## PORTRAITS OF OLDER GARDENS

Alan Emmet

A garden is probably the most fragile, the most perishable form of art. When its maker or its caretaker is no longer able to provide the attention it needs, the garden will soon disappear. The site itself may eventually succumb, paved over, or built upon. How many remarkable residential landscapes have come and gone during the last few centuries in New England alone? We'll never know.

We can read about some of these lost gardens, but pictures can give us a far better view of them. Rare images portray estates of the landed gentry at the dawn of the nineteenth century. We can glimpse these gardens in oil paintings or in drawings by both known and unknown artists. The Lilacs, Thomas Kidder's country seat in Medford, Massachusetts, is depicted in c. 1808 watercolor drawings that provide a detailed picture of the estate, including its circular parterre and a weeping willow, a then newly popular tree. The land at the rear of the house was terraced and cultivated with fruit trees and a vegetable garden (pages 98–99).

*Boston Harbor from Mr. Greene's House, Pemberton Hill*, a massive 1829 oil painting by Robert Salmon, shows the estate of Boston merchant Gardiner Greene, with its terraces of flowers and fruit trees. In his c. 1834 painting, *The House of Gardiner Greene*, now in the collection of the Boston Athenaeum, artist Henry Cheever Pratt provides a view of the front of the Greene mansion, which also includes one of the estate's greenhouses (pages 100–101).

Surveyors' plans also can help us visualize domestic landscapes. John Groves Hales's 1812 plan of the garden at Rundlet-May House (1807) in Portsmouth, New Hampshire, records the gravel walks, plant beds, and orchard. This high-style residential landscape is a rare survivor, with its structure and layout still intact (pages 102–103).

The "picturesque" landscape became fashionable in New England, reflecting the influence of English designers like Lancelot "Capability" Brown and William Kent. The Vale, Theodore Lyman's 1793 picturesque estate in Waltham, Massachusetts, survives to a certain extent in reality, but more completely in a c. 1825 watercolor by Alvan Fisher and in an anonymous painting from the 1830s (pages 104–105).

The big change—a revolutionary change—arrived with the advent of the first commercially successful photographic process in 1839. The camera made it possible to more quickly capture images of a wide variety of gardens – modest and simple places as well as the ornate and grand, and even the most eccentric gardens. Stereo views became ubiquitous from the 1860s to the turn of the twentieth century. These images make it possible to *see* lost gardens in three dimensions.

Stereo views are all that survive of Joseph S. Potter's hillside garden in Arlington, Massachusetts. Its cascades, serpentine ponds, and three-story viewing tower were attractions for the many visitors whom Mr. Potter welcomed (pages 106–107). From 1865 to 1870, Potter compiled an album of photographs, now in the collection of the Boston Athenaeum, to document his garden.

Period photographs are invaluable resources for surviving historic gardens. Current owners and keepers can see how a place used to look, whether or not they wish or are able to make it look as it once did. Trees and shrubs grow or decline, plants die, wooden structures decay. Maintenance may prove the biggest hurdle of all. The grand estate gardens of the nineteenth and early twentieth centuries were designed when it was assumed that plenty of paid professional gardeners would be there to keep them all in perfect order.

The garden at the Hunnewell Estate in Wellesley, Massachusetts, developed in the 1850s and a remarkable survivor to this day, once held 250 topiary trees on its terraced slopes (pages 108–109). Early photographs depict the geometric perfection achieved by five men spending two months each year on long ladders clipping the trees.

Henry Bowen surely had plenty of help to maintain the elaborate boxwood-edged parterre garden at his 1846 Gothic Revival Roseland Cottage in Woodstock, Connecticut. Old photographs and watercolors illustrate the twenty-one small flower beds, outlined as they still are by 600 yards of dwarf English boxwood (pages 110–111).

For years the Codman family at their c. 1740 estate in Lincoln, Massachusetts, had a farmer as well as two full-time gardeners. Thomas Codman took dozens of photographs of the place, including the new Italian Garden that his mother, Sarah, developed and labored over at the turn of the twentieth century. Sarah painted charming watercolors of her beloved home and its grounds. Sarah's daughter Dorothy, also a gardener, made a cottage garden of her own on the estate (pages 112–113).

Others, too, captured garden views with pencil or paint. The artist Childe Hassam painted watercolors of writer Celia Thaxter's colorful flower garden on Appledore Island in the Isles of Shoals off the coast of Maine, adding to its luster and renown. Thaxter maintained her garden from the 1870s until her death in 1894. That year saw the publication of her book, *An Island Garden*, lavishly illustrated by Hassam's watercolors, which has remained enduringly popular (page 94).

By the end of the nineteenth century industrial barons wanted their country estates to reflect their wealth. Frederick Law Olmsted, who established his office adjacent to his Brookline, Massachusetts, home, designed serene landscape settings in the 1880s for homeowners like his neighbors Barthold and Mary McBurney Schlesinger. At Southwood, the Schlesinger's twenty-two acre estate, Olmsted laid out sweeping lawns and meadows, shaded by ancient oaks and other trees. Well-known Boston architectural and marine photographer N. L. Stebbins documented the house and grounds in 1900 in a portfolio of twenty-three striking images (pages 114–115).

Among the very rich the mania for grandiose country estates persisted well into the twentieth century. Charles Adams Platt designed grand houses in ornate landscape settings inspired by European archetypes, especially the Italian Renaissance, including the elaborate adjoining Brookline estates: Larz and Isabel Anderson's Weld (pages 116–117) and Charles Sprague's Faulkner Farm (pages 22–23:41).

These grand places were often photographed by the leading practioners of the day for publication in books and magazines. Prominent professionals like Frances Benjamin Johnston, Mattie Edwards Hewitt, T. E. Marr and Sons, Samuel Gottscho, and others took pictures of gardens for books such as Guy Lowell's *American Gardens* (1902), Louise Shelton's *Beautiful Gardens in America* (1915), and *Monograph of the Work of Charles A. Platt* (1913), and for an expanding roster of magazines, including, *Architectural Record, Country Life in America, The Century Magazine, Better Homes and Gardens, Horticulture,* and *House & Garden.*

Even if their pockets were sufficiently deep, not everyone wanted such formal splendor. When

Emily Tyson and her stepdaughter, Elise, acquired the c. 1785 Hamilton House in South Berwick, Maine, in 1898, they wanted a garden that would suit their old house (pages 118–119). Architect Herbert W. C. Browne of the Boston firm Little and Browne helped them make a Colonial Revival garden, filled with "old-fashioned" flowers. Architectural photographer Paul Weber beautifully captured the garden and house in a series of more than forty images. Weber's photographs illustrated four articles about the property that appeared in *The House Beautiful* in 1929.

The work of landscape architect Fletcher Steele, at Mabel Choate's Stockbridge, Massachusetts, estate, Naumkeag (now a property of The Trustees), has been recorded over and over again by both professional and amateur photographers. Steele, who brought an entirely new approach to gardens, began at Naumkeag in 1926 and worked there for three decades creating the famous Blue Steps, serpentine paths, and patterns meant to be viewed from above (pages 120–121).

Photography has remained the most popular way to preserve the image of a garden at its peak, but the uninhabited pictures of the professional are being eclipsed by the well-populated shots of the amateur (pages 122–123). More gardens are now being photographed than ever before, thanks to the advent of smartphone cameras with superb lenses that can produce razor-sharp views of lovely scenes at almost any time of day with friends or family members in the foreground. Selfies have also become the favorite means for demonstrating a gardener's pride, smiling amidst her most beautiful blossoms.

2

3

4

**The Lilacs**

THE KIDDER ESTATE

*Medford, Massachusetts*

LOST

**Gardiner Greene's House and Garden**

*Boston, Massachusetts*

⬱ LOST ⬱

**Rundlet-May House**

*Portsmouth, New Hampshire*

*Contents*

Nº

1. Manfion Houfe, Green &c.

2. Garden

3. Lot

4.5 Yard, Stable &c:

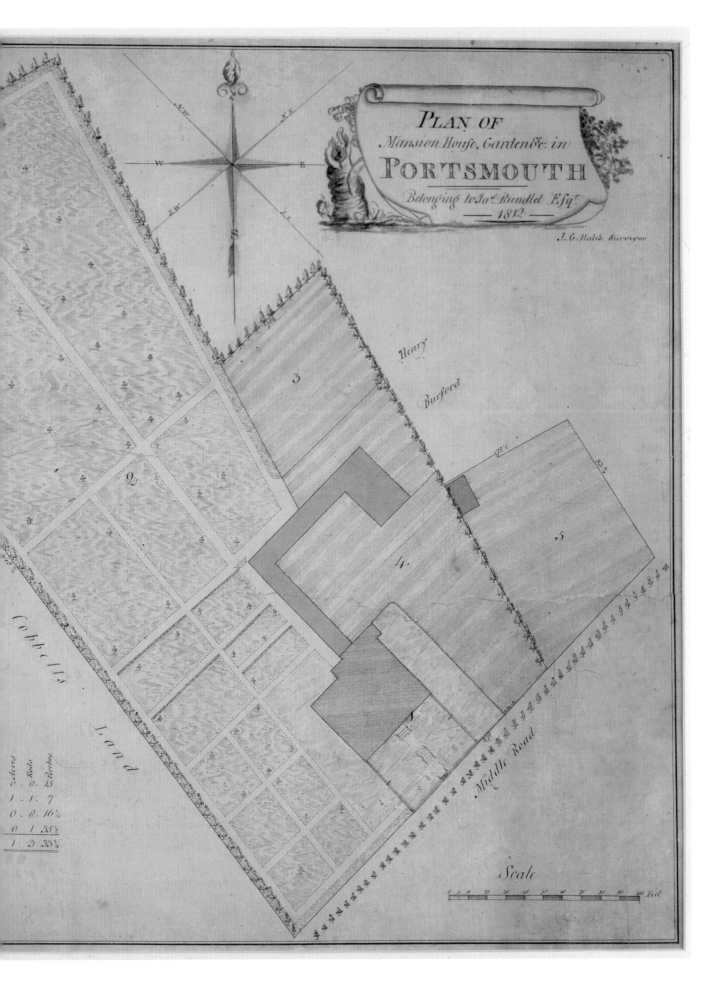

PLAN OF
*Mansion House, Garden &c. in*
**PORTSMOUTH**
*Belonging to Jas. Rundlet Esqr.*
— *1812* —

J. G. Hales, Surveyor

Scale

11

12

13

**Lyman Estate**
*Waltham, Massachusetts*

14

15

16

17

G. K. Proctor, 206 Essex Street, Salem, Mass.

American Views.

18

AMERICAN VIEWS.

182 Essex Street, J. S. MOULTON, Salem, Mass.

C. A. BECKFORD, 141 ESSEX STREET, SALEM, MASS.

W. & J. NO 7 NORTH STR

19

AMERICAN VIEWS.

Potter's Grove

*Arlington, Massachusetts*

LOST

OVERLEAF: 20–32 >

BOSTON AND VICINITY

**Hunnewell Estate**
*Wellesley, Massachusetts*

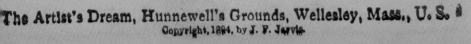

The Artist's Dream, Hunnewell's Grounds, Wellesley, Mass., U. S. A.
Copyright, 1894, by J. F. Jarvis.

34

33

**Roseland Cottage**
*Woodstock, Connecticut*

35

**Codman Estate**
*Lincoln, Massachusetts*

36

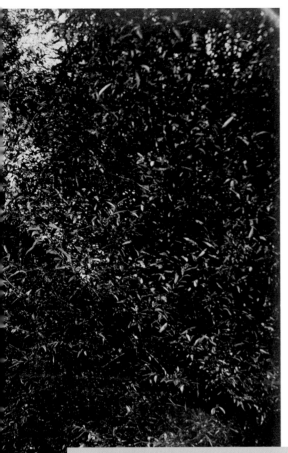

## 37

38

39

**Southwood**

SCHLESINGER ESTATE

*Brookline, Massachusetts*

42

43

Weld

LARZ AND ISABEL ANDERSON ESTATE

*Brookline, Massachusetts*

❧ LOST ❧

44

45

**Hamilton House**
*South Berwick, Maine*

47

**Naumkeag**
*Stockbridge, Massachusetts*

49

50

51

More gardens are now being photographed than
ever before, thanks to the advent of easy-to-use
smartphone cameras. The uninhabited, formal
views of the professional are being eclipsed by
the well-populated shots of the amateur.

52

53

54

1

2

Education has always been a central purpose of garden clubs, ranging from self-education through reading and discussion to public education projects, such as the demonstration gardens that more than 2,500 garden club members helped to design and install at the Horticultural Exhibition at the 1939 New York World's Fair.

# AN UNEXPECTED STORY

## SOCIAL REVOLUTION AND THE GARDEN CLUB

Virginia Lopez Begg

Garden clubs have long been cast as a miscellany of women holding teacups and tinkering with flowers. This negative view has clung although the reality of the garden club movement is very different. Garden clubs were born of revolution, a revolution that changed American women and the landscape of America itself.

From ancient times, farming and gardening were exhausting work though vital to survival. The Industrial Revolution of the nineteenth century prompted many people to leave farms for factories and offices. With this vast social change, the labor of women in the soil became unnecessary for a rising middle class. In fact, it became a source of shame: a woman working in the soil was a red flag indicating that her family was not doing well.

Victorian women, although still busy with household duties, now had some time for other pursuits, especially reading. The onset of the Civil War, however, drew many women from their homes to join in the urgent task of producing supplies for soldiers. As they worked together in sewing, canning, and raising money, women realized the usefulness of such organized groups and the personal satisfaction they offered. After the war, many sought to continue such meaningful activity. A few took the controversial step of founding women's clubs. At that time, the word club signified a male preserve. To associate clubs with respectable women was repugnant. Although growth was slow at first, women's clubs formed across the country, gradually winning acceptance. The clubs' purposes were many but self-education through study and discussion was prominent. By 1890, enough clubs existed to form a national group, the General Federation of Women's Clubs.

The activities of these clubs did not include gardening. Women enjoyed gardens but rejected the actual work of gardening. One female writer commented that women "hold up their hands in holy horror at the very idea of any of their kindred soiling their hands with the work. . . . Yet how much harder do they work at the crowded party or ball!" Others expressed similar thoughts. A committee of the Massachusetts Horticultural Society visited the garden of Mrs. Franklin B. Fay, cultivated "with her own hand." A member noted, "What pity that so few of the ladies of our land imitate her example."

The growth of women's clubs occurred at a time of great change in America. Women's right to vote became an increasingly hot topic. Inventions once scarcely dreamed of altered life dramatically. Yet in the wake of progress there trailed social ills and environmental squalor. A reaction against this dark side of industrialization emerged. The mass production of affordable goods eventually brought about a new appreciation for the pre-industrial craftsmanship then being lost. The nation's centennial in 1876 showcased new technology but also paid homage to the country's past with its emphasis on the work of human hands, leading to the Colonial Revival as many people began to focus on saving historic buildings and landscapes. In the garden, this movement stimulated interest in old-fashioned flowers and gardens, especially among women. As a consequence, Victorian gardens with their hundreds of identical annuals arranged in startling arabesques and rigid geometrical forms began to pass out of favor, along with show-stopping tropical specimens, now deemed unnatural. By the 1890s, unadorned nature had begun to capture the attention of many, including women.

Interest in nature—birds, native plants—drew many women outdoors to explore and study. These women read avidly, and magazine articles and books by reputable female writers focused on this new enthusiasm. Such literature seemed to give permission to the New Woman to abandon Victorian ways. From this cauldron of social change a novel emerged, causing an international sensation, particularly among those who ascribed to the New Woman ideal.

*Elizabeth and Her German Garden*, published anonymously in 1898, was a captivating inside look at aristocracy. The English author said things ladies just did not say. Elizabeth expressed her frustration with family and household duties amusingly. She went on to describe her refuge, her personal space—her garden. The book was an immediate best seller and planted the garden-loving seed in many American women.

Three years later an American book appeared, Helena Rutherfurd Ely's *A Woman's Hardy Garden*. Chatty and conversational, Ely described the how-to information women needed if they were going to garden. Ely had the best of social credentials, making gardening acceptable to many of her readers. She even mentioned manure. The use of the word and the very concept itself marked a sea change for American women. Gardening became an integral part of the revolution taking place in the lives of many. The marriage of gardening and the women's club movement seemed almost inevitable.

A few garden clubs already existed in Georgia, Massachusetts, New York, and some other states. These local clubs did not ignite a wider movement. The national garden club movement really began with the founding of the Garden Club of Philadelphia in 1904. A few friends gathered to share their garden knowledge and soon organized a club. Others heard of it or were already doing the same thing. New clubs organized rapidly and in 1913, the Garden Club of Philadelphia invited eleven other clubs to form an association. This was the birth of the Garden Club of America.

From its beginning, member clubs of the Garden Club of America were composed of socially elite women. As garden clubs formed, they sought to join the GCA. The GCA, however, made the decision to restrict admission. American women, now long experienced in organizing, were not deterred by this policy. One energetic woman in New York, Frances Johnston Paris, organized a garden club in the newly suburban community of Flushing, founded a coalition of Long Island clubs, and in 1924 established the New York State Federation of Garden Clubs, the first such state group in the country. She was a moving force in the 1929 founding of the national group of state federations known today as National Garden Clubs Inc. At its peak, the garden club movement included over half a million American women.

What did this veritable army of gardening women do? Horticulture—learning about plants and how to grow them—was a major focus, for their own gardens and then, increasingly, in the wider community on the local, state, and even national level. Landscape design—the organization of outdoor space to perform a function and do it attractively—captured much attention on both residential and public scales. Horticulture and landscape design in all their aspects were the subjects of many garden club meetings. This provided an attentive audience for the many women and men who became professionals in both areas. Their careers, and incomes, grew through lecturing to garden clubs and writing for garden periodicals and books. Other professions expanded markedly as a result of the garden club movement. From nursery owners and plant specialists to photographers, illustrators, and sculptors, the impact of garden clubs and their members rippled far into the culture and the economy.

As the garden club movement matured, its range of activities expanded rapidly—the numerous shows and exhibitions of plants, floral arrangements, and garden designs held across the country are the most familiar to the wider public. Horticultural societies, such as those of Massachusetts and Pennsylvania, also sponsored shows. These shows have influenced garden trends, stimulating a significant economic impact. From rock gardens and herb gardens in the 1930s to the more recent enthusiasm for perennial gardens, garden club shows have impacted backyards and public spaces throughout America.

Garden clubs have also organized tours and open garden days across the country, increasing public awareness of horticulture, landscape design, and environmental issues as well as historic gardens. Historic Garden Week, held by the Garden Club of Virginia each year, is a well-known example. Funds raised by these events support the maintenance or restoration of historic landscapes and other civic projects throughout the country. Historic American gardens have also been documented by garden club publications. Perhaps the most notable example is the large two-volume *Gardens of Colony and State*, first published in the 1930s by the Garden Club of America, which recorded historic gardens from Massachusetts to California.

Garden clubs looked to the future as well. When America enthusiastically embraced the automobile after World War I, a network of new roads was flung across the landscape. These were soon blotched by billboards everywhere. Garden clubs were among the leaders in seeking to control this blight through relentless publicity campaigns and lobbying lawmakers. Highway beautification has been another club focus, and many miles of plantings have been installed.

The conservation of native plants and places of environmental or scenic importance is another ongoing effort of garden clubs. Garden clubs used educational exhibitions at flower shows and pressured commercial interests to slow the destruction of wildflowers and evergreens. As the irreplaceable California redwoods were logged over, among those who stepped forward in the 1930s with funds to preserve this national treasure was the Garden Club of America. Its redwood grove now includes more than 5,100 acres.

Whether engaged in civic work or home gardening, garden clubs had an equally profound effect on members. As committee chairs and board members of their clubs, many women learned about organizational structure, accounting, publishing, parliamentary procedure, lobbying legislators, and more. Those who sought to move up in the administrative structure to the regional, state, and national levels of National Garden Clubs and the Garden Club of America found themselves running organizations on the scale of many businesses. This experience was invaluable personally and professionally as women increasingly moved into the paid labor force. The garden club movement helped to transform the landscape of America and the women of America. It has played a noteworthy part in shaping women's roles in American history.

3

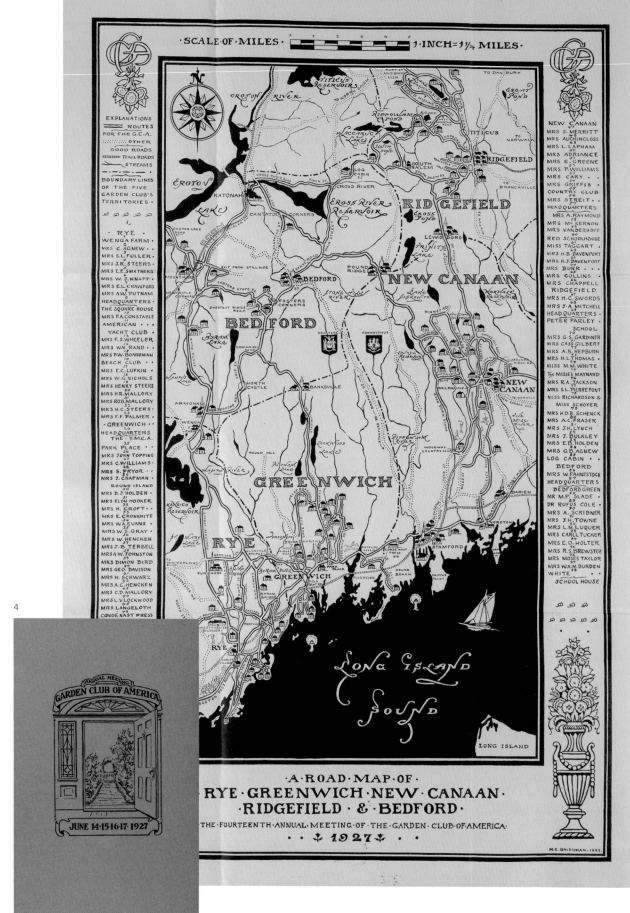

4

# GARDENS
## OF
## COLONY AND STATE

GARDENS AND GARDENERS OF THE AMERICAN
COLONIES AND OF THE REPUBLIC BEFORE 1840

INTRODUCTION · MASSACHUSETTS · CONNECTICUT
MAINE · NEW HAMPSHIRE · VERMONT · RHODE ISLAND
NEW YORK · NEW JERSEY · PENNSYLVANIA · MICHIGAN
OHIO · ILLINOIS · FENCES AND ENCLOSURES

COMPILED AND EDITED FOR
THE GARDEN CLUB OF AMERICA
BY
ALICE G · B · LOCKWOOD
CHAIRMAN
SPECIAL PUBLICATIONS COMMITTEE

5

6

◄ C O N S E R V A T I O N ►

*Education          Planning          Preservation*

### *Foreword*

The purpose of this *Guide* is to supply source
material on conservation and to offer suggestions and
programs to conservation chairmen of Garden Clubs
and to other persons and organizations interested.

In its preparation, an endeavor has been made to
provide a substantially complete and comprehensive
list of the many conservation subjects, not with the
idea that individuals or Garden Clubs will carry on
all the activities mentioned, but that they may select
particular projects on which to concentrate from time
to time.

*The Committee wishes to express its appreciation to all
who have so kindly furnished material used in this Conservation Guide and who have assisted in its preparation.*

Illustrations by ROGER T. PETERSON

For additional copies, inquire of the
CONSERVATION   COMMITTEE

THE   GARDEN   CLUB   OF   AMERICA
598 Madison Avenue, New York City

7

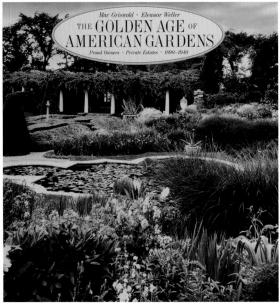

8

Established in 1913, the Garden Club of America continues to be
very active today, holding annual meetings and organizing garden tours, increasing public awareness of horticulture, landscape
design, and environmental issues through educational programs
and exhibitions, preserving natural scenery, and documenting
historic American gardens with major publications.

9

One of the favorite public activities of garden clubs and horticultural societies is the sponsorship of numerous shows and exhibitions of plants, floral arrangements, and garden design held across the country. The annual Spring Flower Show in Boston was one of the most elaborate.

10

11

A GUIDE
to the
SPRING
FLOWER EXHIBITION
of the
MASSACHUSETTS
HORTICULTURAL SOCIETY
[GARDEN CLUBS CO-OPERATING]
MECHANICS BUILDING

MARCH 17—21, 1931

12

OFFICIAL
PROGRAM
OF THE
65th ANNUAL
Spring Flower Show
BOSTON, MASS.

Mechanics Building
MARCH
23, 24, 25, 26, 27, 28
1936

Spring
Flower
Show

Massachusetts
Horticultural
Society
•
Mechanics Bldg.
Boston, Mass.

CERTIFICATE OF LIFE MEMBERSHIP

MARCH 18 to 23, 1946, inclusive

NOT TO BE TAKEN UP AT DOOR

ADM.

N⁰ 223                    Tax

13

14

Massachusetts Horticultural Society
SPRING FLOWER SHOW
Mechanics Building          Boston, Mass.
MARCH 9 to 15 (inclusive), 1952

MEMBER'S ADMISSION TICKET

05957    ADMIT ONE
Tax Exempt
DIRECTOR OF EXHIBITIONS

## 17

15

16

At its peak, the garden club movement included more than half a million American women. In Boston, members of the Flower Club of the Ebenezer Baptist Church posed for a photograph in 1946 (15). Louisa Yeomans King (center, dark coat), known as the "godmother" of the garden club movement, was photographed with members of the Garden Club of Michigan in 1927 (16). The Garden Club of Virginia and its local chapters host an annual tour every April, Garden Week in Virginia, to support the maintenance, restoration, or documentation of historic landscapes throughout the state.

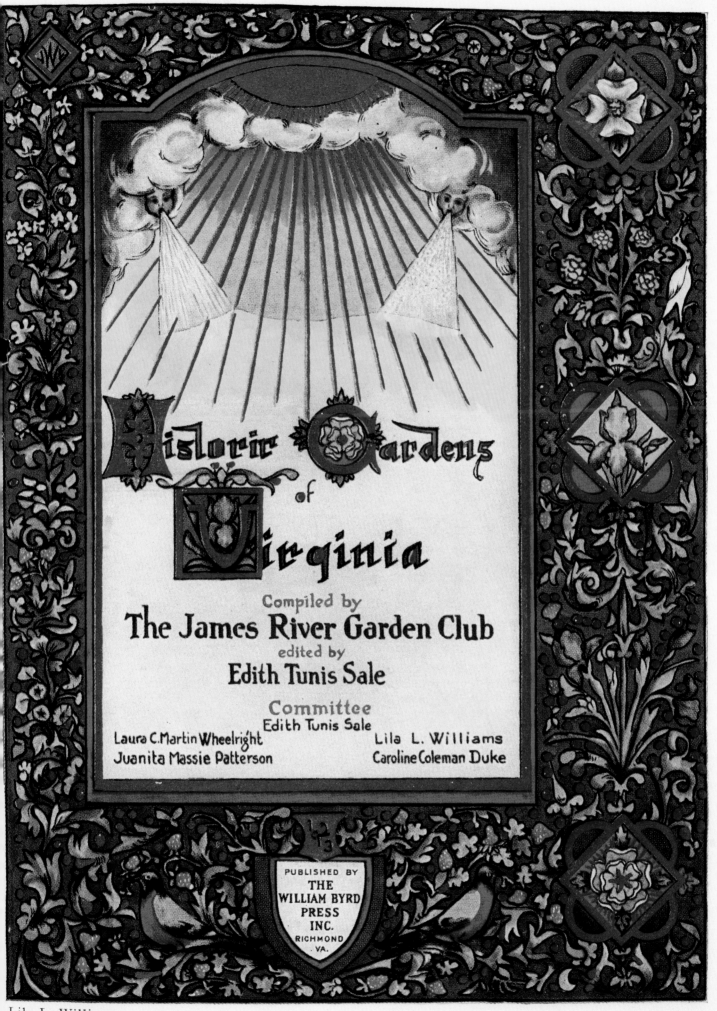

# Historic Gardens of Virginia

of

# Virginia

Compiled by

## The James River Garden Club

edited by

## Edith Tunis Sale

Committee

Edith Tunis Sale

Laura C. Martin Wheelright      Lila L. Williams

Juanita Massie Patterson      Caroline Coleman Duke

PUBLISHED BY
THE
WILLIAM BYRD
PRESS
INC.
RICHMOND
VA.

Lila L. Williams

First Prize
International Flower Show, New York, 1935
won by
Mrs. Henry G. Vaughan

## 18

23

19–22

FIRST PRIZE

RHODE ISLAND FEDERATION OF GARDEN INC.

THIRD PRIZE

NORTH ANDOVER GARDEN CLUB 1930

Second Prize

NORTH ANDOVER GARDEN CLUB 1933

CREATIVITY

FLOWER SHOW AWARD

FIRST AWARD

AMERICA THE BEAUTIFUL

Mrs. Ernest K. Landsteiner

24

Friendly competitions have always been a popular method of encouraging creativity in floral design among garden club members. Winners receive ribbons and citations for the best arrangements from a panel of judges.

# Selected Readings

Benson, Albert Emerson. *History of the Massachusetts Horticultural Society.* Norwood, Mass.: Plimpton Press: Massachusetts Horticultural Society, 1929.

Beveridge, Charles E. and Paul Rocheleau. *Frederick Law Olmsted: Designing the American Landscape.* New York: Rizzoli, 2005. First published 1995.

Birnbaum, Charles A., ed. *Pioneers of American Landscape Design: An Annotated Bibliography.* New York: McGraw-Hill, 1993.

Clayton, Virginia Tuttle. *The Once and Future Gardener: Garden Writing from the Golden Age of Magazines.* Boston: David R. Godine, 2000.

Ellwood, Philip Homer. *American Landscape Architecture.* New York: Architectural Book Publishing, [1924].

Emmet, Alan. *So Fine a Prospect: Historic New England Gardens.* Hanover, N. H. and London: University Press of New England, 1996.

Gilbert, Alma M. and Judith B. Tankard. *A Place of Beauty: The Artists and Gardens of the Cornish Colony.* Berkeley, Calif.: Ten Speed Press, 2000.

Griswold, Mac and Eleanor Weller. *The Golden Age of American Gardens: Proud Owners, Private Estates, 1890–1940.* New York and London: Harry N. Abrams, 2000.

Hill, May Brawley. *Grandmother's Garden: The Old-Fashioned American Garden, 1865–1915.* New York: Harry N. Abrams, 1995.

Hutcheson, Martha Brookes Brown. *The Spirit of the Garden.* Boston: Atlantic Monthly Press, 1923.

King, Mrs. Francis. *The Well-Considered Garden.* New York: Charles Scribner's Sons, 1915.

Mawson, Thomas H. *The Art and Craft of Garden Making.* London: B. T. Batsford, 1900.

Punch, Walter T., ed. *Keeping Eden: A History of Gardening in America.* Boston: Little, Brown, 1992.

Sutton, S. B. *Charles Sprague Sargent and the Arnold Arboretum.* Cambridge, Mass.: Harvard University Press, 2014. First published 1970.

Tankard, Judith B. *Gardens of the Arts & Crafts Movement.* Portland, Ore.: Timber Press, revised ed., 2018.

Thaxter, Celia. *An Island Garden.* Boston: Houghton Mifflin, 1988. First published 1894.

Warren, Arete Swartz. *Gardening by the Book: Celebrating 100 Years of the Garden Club of America.* New York: Garden Club of America; Grolier Club, 2013.

# Illustration Sources

## OPENING ILLUSTRATIONS

PAGE 1. Illustration from catalogue, *Weathervanes by Todhunter* (New York: Arthur Todhunter, 1924.)

PAGE 2. Cover of *Garden & Home Builder*, January 1926.

PAGE 4. Frontispiece depicting the "Country Place of Professor Charles S. Sargent, Brookline, Mass." by Hobart Nichols from *The Lure of the Garden* by Hildegarde Hawthorne (New York: The Century Co., 1911.)

PAGE 6. The cover of *The American Flower Garden* by Neltje Blanchan (New York: Doubleday, Page, 1909.)

PAGE 8. Plate LXV from *The Mayflower*, vol. XI.

PAGE 10. Trade card for Bay State Fertilizer (New Bedford, Mass.: Clark's Cove Guano, 1886.)

PAGE 11. Decorative border from title page of *Little Gardens for Boys and Girls* by Myrta Margaret Higgins (Boston and New York: Houghton Mifflin, 1910.)

## *Reading the Garden: Books and Magazines for Green Thumbs* by Judith B. Tankard

### PAGES 12–35

1. Cover of *The House Beautiful*, June 1916.
2. Illustration from *The Art and Craft of Garden Making* by Thomas H. Mawson (London: B. T. Batsford, fourth ed., 1912.)
3. Title page from *The American Gardener's Calendar* by Bernard M'Mahon (Philadelphia: B. Graves, 1806.)
4. Frontispiece from *A Treatise on the Theory and Practice of Landscape Gardening* by A. J. Downing (New York and London: Wiley and Putnam, second ed., 1844.)
5. Advertisements in *The American Flower Garden Companion* by Edward Sayers (Boston: Joseph Breck, 1838.)
6. Fold out "Plan for Laying Out a Country Place" from *Country Life: A Handbook of Agriculture, Horticulture, and Landscape Gardening* by R. Morris Copeland (Boston: John P. Jewett, 1859.)
7. Plate XXII, "Designs for Neighboring Homes with connecting Grounds," in *The Art of Beautifying Suburban Home Grounds* by Frank J. Scott (New York: D. Appleton, 1870.)
8. A Chart Showing the Colors of Garden Flowers from *The Garden Month by Month* by Mabel Cabot Sedgwick (New York: Frederick A. Stokes, 1907.)
9. Cover of *A Woman's Hardy Garden* by Helena Rutherfurd Ely (New York: Macmillan, 1904.)
10. Cover of *Flower Gardening* by H. S. Adams (New York: McBride, Nast, 1913.)
11. Cover of *How to Lay Out Suburban Home Grounds* by Herbert J. Kellaway (New York: John Wiley and Sons; London: Chapman and Hall, second ed., 1915.)
12. Cover of *The Well-Considered Garden* by Mrs. Francis King [Louisa Boyd Yeomans King] (New York: Charles Scribner's Sons, 1915.)
13. Cover of *Colour in My Garden* by Louise Beebe Wilder (Garden City, N. Y.: Doubleday, Page, 1918.)
14. Cover of *Little Gardens* by Charles M. Skinner (New York: D. Appleton, 1904.)
15. Cover of *The Garden, You, and I* by Mabel Osgood Wright (New York and London: Macmillan, 1906.)
16. Cover of *Sun-Dials and Roses of Yesterday* by Alice Morse Earle (New York and London: Macmillan, 1902.)
17. Cover of *The Garden Book of California* by Belle Sumner Angier (San Francisco and New York: Paul Elder, 1906.)
18. Cover of *Four Seasons in the Garden* by Eben E. Rexford (Philadelphia and London: J. B. Lippincott, 1907.)
19. Cover of *The Joy of Gardens* by Lena May McCauley (Chicago and New York: Rand McNally, 1911.)
20. Cover of *Beautiful Gardens in America* by Louise Shelton (New York: Charles Scribner's Sons, 1915.)
21. Detail of the cover of *Old Time Gardens* by Alice Morse Earle (New York: Macmillan, 1901.)
22. Cover of *The Seasons in a Flower Garden* by Louise Shelton (New York: Charles Scribner's Sons, 1906.)
23. Cover of *Amateur Gardencraft* by Eben E. Rexford (Philadelphia and London: J. B. Lippincott, 1912.)
24. Cover of *Gardens Near the Sea* by Alice Lounsberry (New York: Frederick A. Stokes, 1910.)
25. Cover of *The Landscape Gardening Book* by Grace Tabor (New York: McBride, Winston, 1911.)
26. Cover of *The Garden of a Commuter's Wife* (New York: Macmillan, sixth ed., 1903.)
27. Cover of *Old Time Gardens* by Alice Morse Earle (New York: Macmillan, 1916.)
28. Photograph of the estate of Charles M. Schwab, Loretto, Pa., from catalogue, *Some Landscape Work of the Philadelphia Branch of*

*Lewis and Valentine Co.* (Ardmore, Pa.: Lewis and Valentine, [n.d.].)

**29.** Cover of *American Gardens* edited by Guy Lowell (Boston: Bates and Guild, 1902.)

**30.** Testimonial letter from E. T. Stotesbury and photograph of his estate, Whitemarsh Hall, in Springfield Township, Pa., from catalogue, *Landscape Planting and Engineering Lewis and Valentine Co.* (New York: Lewis and Valentine, [c. 1922].)

**31.** Cover of *Art-Out-of-Doors: Hints on Good Taste in Gardening* by Mrs. Schuyler Van Rensselaer [Mariana Van Rensselaer] (New York: Charles Scribner's Sons, 1893.)

**32.** Cover of *Spanish Gardens and Patios* by Mildred Stapley Byne and Arthur Byne (Philadelphia and London: J. P. Lippincott; New York: The Architectural Record, 1928.)

**33.** Title page of *China: Mother of Gardens* by Ernest H. Wilson (Boston: Stratford Co., 1929.)

**34.** Cover of *American Estates and Gardens* by Barr Ferree (New York: Munn, 1906.)

**35.** Frontispiece depicting "Hedge Walk, Quirinal Gardens" by Charles A. Platt from *Italian Gardens* by Charles A. Platt (New York: Harper & Brothers, 1894.)

**36.** Cover of *The House Beautiful*, September 1909.

**37.** Cover of *Architectural Gardens of Italy: A Series of Photogravure Plates from Photographs made for and selected by A. Holland Forbes* (New York: Forbes, 1902.)

**38.** Cover of *Italian Villas and Their Gardens* by Edith Wharton (New York: The Century Co., 1907.)

**39.** Cover of *The Gardens of Italy* by Charles Latham (London: Country Life; New York: Charles Scribner's Sons, 1905.)

**40.** Cover of *Italian Gardens* by Charles A. Platt (New York: Harper & Brothers, 1894.)

**41.** Photograph of "Faulkner Farm—The Pool before the Casino" from *American Estates and Gardens* by Barr Ferree (New York: Munn, 1904.)

**42–51.** Covers of: *Country Life in America*, April 1932; *The Ladies' Home Journal*, June 1909; *House & Garden*, October 1915; *House & Garden*, March 1929; *The Garden Magazine*, February to July 1906; *House Beautiful*, April 1924; *Indoors and Out*, July 1906; *American Homes and Gardens*, January 1906; *The Craftsman*, May 1913; *The House Beautiful*, March 1916.

**52.** Frontispiece depicting "Combe in west country with primroses, kingcups, and daffodils" by Alfred Parsons from *The Wild Garden* by W. Robinson (London: John Murray, fourth ed., 1894.)

**53.** Spines of Gertrude Jekyll's books: *Wood and Garden* (London, New York, Bombay, and Calcutta: Longmans, Green, 1910); *Colour in the Flower Garden* (London: Country Life and George Newnes, 1908); *Old West Surrey* (London, New York, and Bombay: Longmans, Green, 1904); *Gardens for Small Country Houses*, with Lawrence Weaver (London: Country Life and George Newnes; New York: Charles Scribner's Sons, second ed., 1913); *Wall and Water Gardens* (London: Country Life and George Newnes, [1901]); *Home and Garden* (London, New York, and Bombay: Longmans, Green, 1900).

**54.** Frontispiece depicting "June Borders of Lupin and Iris in the Garden at Munstead Wood" from *Gardens for Small Country Houses* by Gertrude Jekyll and Lawrence Weaver (London: Country Life and George Newnes; New York: Charles Scribner's Sons, second ed., 1913.)

**55.** Photograph of Hardwick Hall, Derbyshire, the Seat of His Grace the Duke of Devonshire from *Gardens Old and New: The Country House & Its Garden Environment* (London: Country Life Illustrated and George Newnes, [n.d.].)

**56.** Cover of *What England Can Teach Us about Gardening* by Wilhelm Miller (Garden City, N. Y.: Doubleday, Page, 1911.)

**57.** Cover of *English Pleasure Gardens* by Rose Standish Nichols (New York and London: Macmillan, 1902.)

**58.** Cover from *Gardens Old and New: The Country House & Its Garden Environment* (London: Country Life Illustrated and George Newnes, [n.d.].)

**59.** Design for a garden in the New England area by Robert Washburn Beal, A.S.L.A., Boston. Ladies' Home Journal Garden Pattern, No. 149 (Philadelphia: Curtis Publishing, 1931.)

**60.** Design for a garden in the New England area by Charles Mowbray Davidson and Stuart Constable, Stamford, Conn. Ladies' Home Journal Garden Pattern, No. 150 (Philadelphia: Curtis Publishing, 1931.)

**61–64.** Covers of envelopes containing Ladies' Home Journal Garden Patterns for the New England States by Fletcher Steele (no. 152); Charles Mowbray Davidson and Stuart Constable (no. 150); Robert Washburn Beal (no. 149); and Harold Hill Blossom (no. 154) (Philadelphia: Curtis Publishing, 1931.)

**65.** Illustration from catalogue, *Landscape Planting and Engineering Lewis and Valentine Co.* (New York: Lewis and Valentine, [c. 1922].)

**66.** Poster, *Follow the Pied Piper* by Maginel Wright Barney (Washington, DC: The Graphic Co., [c. 1918].)

**67.** Illustration after J. N. Darling, back cover of pamphlet, *War Gardening and Home Storage of Vegetables* (Washington DC: National War Garden Commission, 1919.)

**68.** Cover of *Have a Victory Garden* by L. A. Hawkins (Chicago: International Harvester, [c. 1943].)

**69.** Illustration from *House Beautiful's Practical Gardener, 1943 Season.*

**70.** Cover of catalogue, *The Spirit of 1943 "Plant and Grow" Wood's Tested Seeds* (Richmond, Va.: T. W. Wood and Sons.)

**71.** Cover of booklet, *A Book of Simple Directions for a Victory Garden* (New York: Ideal Distributing, 1943.)

**72, 74.** Illustration from and cover of *Little Gardens for Boys and Girls* by Myrta Margaret Higgins (Boston and New York: Houghton Mifflin, 1910.)

**73, 75.** Cover of and illustration from *A Flower Fairy Alphabet* by Cicely Mary Barker (London and Glasgow: Blackie and Son, 1934.)

**76, 77.** Illustration by Charles Robinson and title page from *The Secret Garden* by Frances Hodgson Burnett (London: William Heinemann, fourth printing, 1914.)

**78–82.** Covers of: *Design in the Little Garden* by Fletcher Steele (Boston: Atlantic Monthly Press, 1924); *The Little Garden* by Mrs. Francis [Louisa Yeomans] King (Boston: Atlantic Monthly Press, third printing, 1922); *Peonies in the Little Garden* by Mrs. Edward [Alice] Harding (Boston: Atlantic Monthly Press, 1923); *Iris in the Little Garden* by Ella Porter McKinney (Boston: Little, Brown, 1927); *Roses in the Little Garden* by G. A. Stevens (Boston: Little, Brown, 1926).

**83.** List of titles in the series, *Handbooks of Practical Gardening*, published in *The Book of the Wild Garden* by S. W. Fitzherbert (London and New York: John Lane, 1903.)

**84.** Inside front cover and title page from *Better Homes & Gardens Garden Book: A Year-Round Guide to Practical Home Gardening* (Des Moines, Iowa: Meredith Publishing, second ed., 1954.)

**85.** Cover of *Taylor's Weekend Gardening Guides: The Cutting Garden* by Rob Proctor (Boston and New York: Houghton Mifflin, 2000.)

**86.** Cover of *Taylor's Weekend Gardening Guides: The Winter Garden* by Rita Buchanan (Boston and New York: Houghton Mifflin, 1997.)

**87.** Cover of *Taylor's Weekend Gardening Guides: Small Gardens* by Glenn Morris (Boston and New York: Houghton Mifflin, 1999.)

**88.** Cover of *The Home Garden*, January 1946.

*Great Expectations: A Cornucopia of Catalogues* by Richard C. Nylander

PAGES 36–67

**1.** Cover of catalogue, *Burpee's Farm Annual, 1892* (Philadelphia: W. Atlee Burpee.)
**2.** Cover of catalogue, *Childs' Rare Flowers, Vegetables & Fruits 1898* (Floral Park, N. Y.: John Lewis Childs.)
**3.** Cover of catalogue, *Farquhar's Catalogue of Seeds, Plants, Bulbs, Tools, Fertilizers, Sundries 1900* (Boston: R. and J. Farquhar.)
**4.** Mailing envelope for forms for ordering seeds (Philadelphia: W. Atlee Burpee, [n.d.].)
**5.** Advertisement for Rice's Seeds (Cambridge, N. Y.: Jerome B. Rice, [1875].)
**6.** Trade card for Vick's Choice Seeds (Rochester, N. Y.: Vick's Seed, [n.d.].) Seeds sold by W. S. Smith and Sons, Binghampton, N. Y.
**7.** Cover of catalogue, *Beautify Your Home and Make Your Garden Bring in Most of Your Living* (Dansville, N. Y.: Reilly Brothers Nurseries, [c. 1915].)
**8.** Illustration from catalogue, *New Ideas in Home Landscaping for 1927* (Framingham Centre, Mass.: Little Tree Farms.)
**9.** Cover of catalogue, *It's Not a Home Until It's Planted* (Rochester, N. Y.: Green's Nursery, 1924.)
**10.** Cover of catalogue, *New Ideas in Home Landscaping for 1927* (Framingham Centre, Mass.: Little Tree Farms.)
**11.** Cover of catalogue, *Beautifying the Home Grounds* (New Orleans: Southern Pine Assoc., 1942.)
**12.** Cover of catalogue, *Permanent Improvements to the Home and Grounds* (Chicago and Allentown, Pa.: Lehigh Portland Cement, [n.d.].)
**13.** Cover of catalogue, *Beautifying the Home Grounds* (New Orleans: Southern Pine Assoc., 1926.)
**14.** Cover of catalogue, *The Book of Lawn Furniture* (Kansas City, Mo.: Long-Bell Lumber, fourth ed., 1927.) Sold by J. W. White Co., Lewiston, Maine.
**15.** Illustration from *Catalogue of Green's Nursery Co., Spring 1896* (Rochester, N. Y.: Green's Nursery.)
**16.** Advertisement for John Kyle's nursery at Indian Hill Farm, West Newbury, Mass., c. 1835. Published in an unidentified newspaper.
**17.** Lithograph of Hovey and Co. seed store, Boston, for *The New England Pictorial Index*, by J. Mayer & Co.
**18–25.** Covers of catalogues: *Catalogue of Green's Nursery Co., Spring 1896* (Rochester, N. Y.: Green's Nursery); *Trees and Plants from Vermont for 1930* (Putney, Vt.: George D. Aiken); *Cherry Hill Nurseries, 1928* (West Newbury, Mass.: T. C. Thurlow's Sons); *Little Tree Farms Year Book for 1922/1923* (Boston: American Forestry); *Hardy Plants for New England Gardens, 1931* (Ward Hill, Mass.: Gray & Cole); *Mahoney's Rocky Ledge Farm & Nursery* (Winchester, Mass.: Mahoney's Garden Center, [n.d.].); *Weston Nurseries* (Weston, Mass., 1933); *The Original Barnes Bros. Nursery* (Yalesville, Conn.: Barnes Bros. Nursery, 1930).
**26.** Display box for seeds, *Lady Mae Seed Co., Greenville, South Carolina, 1922.*
**27.** Seed packet for *Shakers' Long Orange Carrot. F. S. Tyringham, Mass.* Courtesy of Communal Societies Collection, Burke Library, Hamilton College.
**28.** Label for green pea seeds (Boston: W. K. Lewis & Brothers, [n.d.].)
**29.** Order form for Seeds for the Children's Gardens (Philadelphia: W. Atlee Burpee, 1913.)
**30.** Illustration from catalogue, *Manual of Everything for the Garden, Jubilee Edition 1897* (New York: Peter Henderson.)
**31.** Trade card for Rice's Seeds (Cambridge, N. Y.: Jerome B. Rice, 1885.)
**32.** Advertisement for Ferry's Seeds (Detroit: D. M. Ferry, 1921.)
**33.** Illustration from catalogue, *Manual of Everything for the Garden, Jubilee Edition 1897* (New York: Peter Henderson.)
**34.** Illustration from *Vick's Floral Guide* (Rochester, N. Y.: James Vick, 1884.)
**35.** Order form from catalogue, *1923 Plant Harts Seeds* (Wethersfield, Conn.: Chas. C. Hart.)
**36.** Cover of catalogue, *Livingston's Seed Annual, 1903* (Columbus, Ohio: A. W. Livingston's.)
**37.** Cover of catalogue, *1923 Plant Harts Seeds* (Wethersfield, Conn.: Chas. C. Hart.)
**38.** Illustration from *The Mayflower*, vol. IX, pl. XXXIV.
**39.** Illustration from *The Mayflower*, vol. X, pl. XL.
**40.** Back cover of catalogue, *Burpee's Annual for 1913* (Philadelphia: W. Atlee Burpee.)
**41.** Illustration from *The Mayflower*, vol. IX, pl. XXXII.
**42.** Back cover of catalogue, *L. L. May & Co., 1898* (St. Paul, Minn.: L. L. May.)
**43.** Illustration from *The Book of Gardens: A Treatise on American and Foreign Bulbs for Outdoor and Indoor Culture* (New York: John Scheepers, 1920.)
**44.** Mailing envelope for *Burpee's Bulbs for Fall Planting 1934* (Philadelphia: W. Atlee Burpee.)
**45.** Label for bulbs (Boston and Cambridge, Mass.: Parker and Gannett, 1882.)
**46.** Illustration from *Illustrated Catalogue, Agricultural Hardware, Implements, Machines and Woodenware* (Boston: Joseph Breck, 1897.)
**47.** Cover of catalogue, *Bradley's Super-Phosphate of Lime, 1884* (Boston: Bradley Fertilizer.) Sold by Eli Morton, White Rock, Maine.
**48.** Trade card for The Currie Fertilizer Co. (Louisville, Ky.: Currie Fertilizer, [n.d.].)
**49-50.** Trade cards for Bay State Fertilizer (New Bedford, Mass.: Clark's Cove Guano, 1886.)
**51.** Illustration from catalogue, *Joseph Breck & Sons, 1896* (Boston: Joseph Breck.)
**52.** Cover of brochure, *Save Your Garden from Insects and Disease* (Arnold Garden Hose Spray, 1937.) Sold by Brecks, Boston.
**53.** Cover of catalogue, *Everything for the Garden 1918* (depicting Westover, Va.) (New York: Peter Henderson.)
**54.** Cover of catalogue, *Everything for the Garden 1932* (depicting Mount Vernon, Va.) (New York: Peter Henderson.)
**55-56.** Illustrations from catalogue, *Garden Furniture of Distinction* (Boston: W. A. Snow Iron Works, [c. 1925].)
**57.** Cover of catalogue, *Everything for the Garden 1933* (depicting Ash Lawn, Va.) (New York: Peter Henderson.)
**58.** Back cover of brochure, *Moto-Mower* (Detroit: Moto-Mower, [c. 1940].) Sold by The Farmstore, Springfield, Mass.
**59.** Illustration from cover of catalogue, *The Ideal Lawn Mower Sharpener* (Plymouth, Ohio: Fate-Root-Heath, [c. 1925].)
**60.** Illustration from *Manual of Everything for the Garden 1899* (New York: Peter Henderson.)
**61.** Circular for *List of Parts and Directions for Use of the Great American Ball Bearing Lawn Mower* (Philadelphia: Pennsylvania Lawn Mower, [n.d.].)
**62.** Trade card for Excelsior Side Wheel Mower (Newburgh, N. Y.: Chadborn & Coldwell, [c. 1875].)
**63.** Trade card for New Champion Force Pump (Belmont, N. Y.: Clark Bros., [c. 1875].) Sold by Phineas White, New Bedford, Mass.
**64.** Illustration from catalogue, *Garden Hose Book* (Cambridge, Mass.: Boston Woven Hose and Rubber, [n.d.].)
**65.** Cover of trade catalogue, *Rain for the Asking* (Troy, Ohio: Skinner Irrigation, [n.d.].)
**66.** Illustration from catalogue, *Manual of Everything for the Garden, Jubilee Edition 1897* (New York: Peter Henderson.)
**67.** Illustration from *Sunset Ideas for Building Plant Shelters and Garden Work Centers* (Menlo Park, Calif.: Lane Publishing, 1953.)
**68.** Illustration from catalogue, *America's Largest Manufacturer of Canvas Products 1935* (Toledo, Ohio: Hettrick Manufacturing.)

**69, 71.** Illustration from and cover of *How to Make an Outdoor Living Room* (Davenport, Iowa: National Home Planting Bureau, 1930.) Sold by J. W. Adams Nursery Co., Westfield, Mass.

**70.** Illustration from brochure, *Walpole Cedar Furniture* (Walpole, Mass.: Walpole Woodworkers, [n.d.].)

**72.** Illustration from *Illustrated Catalogue, Agricultural Hardware, Implements, Machines and Woodenware* (Boston: Joseph Breck, 1897.)

**73.** Illustration from brochure, *Arvin Metal Outdoor Furniture* (Columbus, Ind.: Arvin Industries, 1952.)

**74.** Cover of catalogue, *Hampden Outdoor Furniture* (Easthampton, Mass.: Hampden Specialty Products, [1950s].)

**75.** Illustration from catalogue, *Gold Medal Folding Furniture for 1933* (Racine, Wis.: Gold Medal Folding Furniture.)

**76.** Cover of brochure, Metalart Outdoor Chairs (Paterson, N. J.: Metalart, [c. 1935].)

**77.** Illustration from catalogue, *White Flower Farm Spring 2018 Garden Book* (Litchfield, Conn.: White Flower Farm.)

**78.** Photograph of the Peggy Rockefeller Rose Garden at the New York Botanical Garden. Photograph by Richard Cheek © 2010.

**79.** Illustration from catalogue, *White Flower Farm Spring 2019 Garden Book* (Litchfield, Conn.: White Flower Farm.)

**80.** Cover of catalogue, *Breck's 2018 Fall Sale* (Guilford, Ind.: Breck's.)

**81.** Cover of catalogue, *Comstock Seeds 2011 Catalog* (Wethersfield, Conn.: Comstock, Ferre.)

**82.** Cover of catalogue, *David Austin Handbook of Roses 2010* (Tyler, Tex.: David Austin Roses.)

### *Beyond the Garden Gate: Art, Architecture, and Ornament* by Richard C. Nylander

PAGES 68–93

**1.** Photograph of the Saltonstall children in their garden, Milton, Mass., c. 1901. Alice Augusta Rogerson Brown, photographer.

**2.** Cover of catalogue, *Anchor-Weld Iron Fences and Gates, Catalog No. 83* (Baltimore, Md.: Anchor Post Fence, 1929.)

**3.** Cover of *The Century Book of Gardening: A Comprehensive Work for Every Lover of the Garden,* edited by E. T. Cook (London: Country Life and George Newnes; New York: Doubleday, Page, 1900.)

**4.** Photograph of the Spaulding Gardens, Beverly Farms, Mass., designed by Little and Browne, architects, c. 1908. Photographer unknown.

**5.** Cover of *The House Beautiful*, March 1909, depicting the garden path, the residence of F. T. Maxwell, Rockville, Conn.

**6.** Photograph of the iris garden and pergola at Iristhorpe Farm, the residence of Homer and Mable Gage, Shrewsbury, Mass., c. 1917. Mary H. Northend, photographer.

**7.** Illustration of "Proposed Fountain-Pond, Pergula and Temple, Shenstone Court," from *The Art and Craft of Garden Making* by Thomas H. Mawson (London: B. T. Batsford, fifth ed., 1926.)

**8.** Photograph of the garden of Gardiner M. Lane, Manchester, Mass., c. 1924. Mary H. Northend, photographer.

**9.** Drawing of a *Trellis for E. L. Winthrop, Esq., Newport, R. I.*, c. 1900. Ogden Codman, architect.

**10.** Photograph of the Lattice Garden Pavilion at William Wharton's, Groton, Mass., n.d. Photographer unknown.

**11, 13.** Illustration from and cover of catalogue, *The Joy of Living Out of Doors* (Saginaw, Mich.: Mershon-Eddy-Parker, [n.d.].)

**12.** Stereo view of an unidentified garden scene with a grapery, possibly Roxbury, Mass., c.1860. Deloss Barnum, photographer.

**14.** Photograph of the Gothic Revival summer house, Barrett House, New Ipswich, N. H. David Bohl, photographer.

**15.** Photograph of children in a gazebo, location unknown, c. 1890. Photographer unknown.

**16.** Photograph of the Garden House, Royall House, Medford, Mass., c. 1900. Wilfred A. French, photographer.

**17.** Summer house designed by Samuel McIntire, Glen Magna, Endicott Estate, Danvers, Mass., c. 1905. Mary H. Northend, photographer.

**18.** Stereo view of the Gothic Revival summer house, Wheelwright garden, Newburyport, Mass., c. 1865. Philip Coombs, photographer.

**19.** Illustration from catalogue, *American Greenhouses* (Brooklyn, N. Y.: American-Moninger Greenhouse Mfg. Co., [1927].)

**20.** Stereo view of the interior of a greenhouse, location unknown, c. 1878. J. W. and J. S. Moulton, photographers.

**21.** Cover of catalogue, *Glass Enclosures* (Irvington, N. Y.: Lord and Burnham, [c. 1930].)

**22.** Detail of cover of catalogue, *Sectional Iron Frame Greenhouses That We Have Designed and Erected* (New York: Lord and Burnham, ninth ed., 1910.)

**23.** Photograph of the greenhouses, Lyman Estate, Waltham, Mass., c. 1884. A. H. Folsom, photographer.

**24.** Cover of catalogue, *American Lawn Fence* (New York: American Steel and Wire, 1929.)

**25.** *Drawing of Fore Court Fence and Gates From Main Avenue, House for H. C. Frick, Esq., Prides, Mass.,* February 6, 1905. Arthur Little and Herbert Browne, architects.

**26.** Illustration from *American Agriculturist for the Farm, Garden, and Household*, July 1877.

**27.** Illustration from catalogue, *The Landscape Art* (Framingham Centre, Mass.: Little-Tree Landscaping and Forestry Service [c. 1928].)

**28.** Cover of catalogue, *Anchor Post Iron Works Catalogue, No. 44, Iron Railings, Wire Fences, Entrance Gates* (New York: Anchor Post Iron Works, [1911].)

**29.** Drawing of a "Brick & Iron Enclosing Fence for Thos. Dreier Estate Winchester, Mass.," including a design for a fountain, 1924. Frank Chouteau Brown, architect.

**30.** Illustration from catalogue, *Ornamental Iron and Zinc Fountains* (New York: J. W. Fiske Iron Works, 1928.)

**31.** Illustration from catalogue, *Galloway Pottery, Catalogue, No. 30* (Philadelphia: Galloway Terra-Cotta, [n.d.].)

**32.** Photograph of a fountain, at Highwood, Walker Residence, Manchester, Mass., c. 1910. Mary H. Northend, photographer.

**33.** Photograph of the fountain at the Bayard Thayer Estate, Lancaster, Mass., c. 1905. Photographer unknown.

**34.** Photograph of Harriot Hopkinson, Hamilton House, South Berwick, Maine, 1908. Elise Tyson [later Vaughan], photographer.

**35.** Illustration from catalogue, *Galloway Pottery, Catalogue, No. 30* (Philadelphia: Galloway Terra-Cotta, [n.d.].)

**36.** Detail of a "Martin House" from a drawing, *Alterations to the House of H. Emerson at Harrison Square in Dorchester, Massachusetts, 1860.* Luther Briggs Jr., architect.

**37.** Illustration from catalogue, *Equipment for Your Suburban and Country Home* (Boston and New York: E. F. Hodgson, 1931.)

**38.** Illustration from *Boy Bird House Architecture* by Leon H. Baxter (Milwaukee: Bruce Publishing, 1920.)

**39.** Illustration from catalogue, *Little-Tree Farms Catalogue and Year Book 41* (Framingham Centre, Mass.: Little-Tree Farms Landscaping and Forestry Service, [n. d.].)

**40.** Cover of *American Homes and Gardens*, September 1907, depicting Mrs. Guy Norman's Sicilian Garden, Beverly, Mass. Herbert Browne, architect.

**41.** Photograph of urn at Rosecliffe, Newport, R. I., 1981. Photograph © Richard Cheek for The Preservation Society of Newport County.

**42.** Photograph of the garden at Hamilton House, South Berwick, Maine, showing the lion head garden planter, 1902. Elise Tyson [later Vaughan], photographer.

**43.** Photograph of the lion head garden

planter from Hamilton House, South Berwick, Maine. David Carmack, photographer.

**44, 48.** Page from and cover of catalogue, *Colorcrete: The New Gateway to Money-making Opportunities* (Holland, Mich.: Colorcrete Industries, [c. 1928].)

**45.** Illustration from catalogue, *Alpha Aids, No. 31* (Easton, Pa. and Chicago: Alpha Portland Cement, [c. 1925].)

**46.** Illustration from catalogue, *Atlas White Portland Cement for Ornamental Cast Work* (New York: Atlas Portland Cement, 1926.)

**47.** Cover of *How to Make Concrete Garden Furniture and Accessories*, edited by John T. Fallon (New York: Robert M. McBride, 1917.)

**49.** Photograph of statues of gnomes and rabbits at Weld, the Larz and Isabel Anderson Estate, Brookline, Mass., before 1941. Photographer unknown.

**50.** Photograph of a pair of Don Featherstone pink flamingos, 2019. Chloe Schoppmeyer, photographer.

**51.** Photograph of *Hadrian's Mother*, Glen Burnie, Winchester, Va., 1992. Photograph © Richard Cheek for the Garden Club of Virginia.

**52.** Photograph of *Dancing Girls* by Mario Korbel in Friendship Pond, Norfolk Botanical Garden, Virginia. Photograph © Richard Cheek for the Garden Club of Virginia.

**53.** Photograph of sundial, Hamilton House, South Berwick, Maine, 2004. Sandy Agrafiotis, photographer.

**54.** Photograph of the garden at Wodenethe, the estate of Henry Winthrop Sargent, Fishkill Landing [now Beacon], N. Y., c. 1910. Alman & Co., photographers.

**55.** Cover of *Yard and Garden* by Tarkington Baker (Indianapolis: Bobbs-Merrill, revised ed., 1913.)

**56.** Illustration from catalogue, *Galloway Pottery, Catalogue, No. 30* (Philadelphia: Galloway Terra-Cotta, [n.d.].)

### Where Flowers Never Fade: Portraits of Older Gardens by Alan Emmet

PAGES 94–123

**1.** Frontispiece from *An Island Garden* by Celia Thaxter, with pictures and illuminations by Childe Hassam (Boston and New York: Houghton Mifflin, 1894.)

**2.** Stereo view of a mirror globe reflecting the photographer, Ridge Hill Farms, Needham, Mass., 1870s. C. Seaver Jr., photographer.

**3–4.** Front and rear views of The Lilacs, the Kidder Estate, Medford, Mass., artist unknown, c. 1808. Watercolor on heavy paper.

**5.** Photograph of the Kidder mansion, c 1905. Photographer unknown.

**6.** *Boston Harbor from Mr. Greene's House,*

*Pemberton Hill* by Robert Salmon, 1829. Tempera on canvas.

**7.** *The House of Gardiner Greene* by Henry Cheever Pratt, c. 1834. Oil on canvas. Boston Athenaeum, Gift of Copley Amory Jr., 1961.

**8.** Photograph of the rose pergola at Rundlet-May House, Portsmouth, N. H. Chandler Simpkins, photographer.

**9.** Photograph of the garden at Rundlet-May House, Portsmouth, N. H. David Bohl, photographer.

**10.** *Plan of Mansion House, Gardens &C. in Portsmouth Belonging to Jas. Rundlet Esqr.* 1812 by J. G. Hales. Ink on paper.

**11.** *The Vale*, c. 1825. Artist unknown. Oil on canvas.

**12.** *The Vale* by Alvan Fisher, c. 1825. Pencil and watercolor on paper.

**13.** Photograph of the Lyman Estate greenhouse, Waltham, Mass. David Bohl, photographer.

**14–19.** Stereo views of Potter's Grove, Arlington, Mass., c. 1870. Photographs by: John S. Moulton (**14**); photographer unknown (**15**); C. A. Beckford (**16**); G. K. Proctor (**17**); J. S. Moulton (**18**); J. W. and J. S. Moulton (**19**).

**20–32.** Stereo views of the Hunnewell Estate, Wellesley, Mass.: *The Artist's Dream, Hunnewell's Grounds, Wellesley, Mass., U.S.,* 1894. J. F. Jarvis, photographer, Underwood and Underwood, publishers (**20**); C. Seaver Jr., photographer, Charles Pollock, publisher, 1872 (**21, 23, 30**); photographer unknown, Charles Pollock, publisher, 1872 (**22, 24, 26–27, 29**); *A Poem to Trees, Hunnewell's Ground, Wellesley, Mass., U.S.A.,* 1894. J. F. Jarvis, photographer, Underwood and Underwood, publishers (**25**); C. Seaver Jr., photographer, c. 1872 (**28**); photographer unknown, American Views publisher, n.d. (**31**); Universal Photo Art Co., C. H. Graves, publisher, 1901 (**32**).

**33.** Photograph of Roseland Cottage, Woodstock, Conn. David Bohl, photographer.

**34.** Photograph of Sylvia Holt, granddaughter of Henry and Lucy Bowen, in the garden at Roseland Cottage, Woodstock, Conn., 1901. Photographer unknown.

**35.** Watercolor of Roseland Cottage, c. 1846. Attributed to Joseph Collins Wells, the architect of the house.

**36.** Photograph of *Lincoln the Garden*, c. 1904. Photograph attributed to Thomas Newbold Codman.

**37.** Photograph of Dorothy Codman in her cottage garden, Lincoln, Mass., 1911. Photographer unknown.

**38.** *View from the House Sept [18]98.* Watercolor of the Codman Estate grounds, Lincoln, Mass., by Sarah Fletcher Bradlee Codman.

**39–40.** Photographs of Southwood, the

Schlesinger Estate, Brookline, Mass., 1900. N. L. Stebbins, photographer.

**41–42.** Photographs of the garden at Weld, the Larz and Isabel Anderson Estate, Brookline, Mass., n.d. Photographer unknown.

**43.** Photograph of the municipal skating rink/tennis court, Brookline, Mass., built on the former site of the garden at the Larz and Isabel Anderson Estate, 1976. Richard Cheek, photographer.

**44.** Photograph of the garden at Hamilton House, South Berwick, Maine, c. 2000. Dana Salvo, photographer.

**45.** Glass slide of the Garden Cottage at Hamilton House, South Berwick, Maine, n.d. From the Smithsonian Institution, Archives of American Gardens, Washington DC, Garden Club of America Collection.

**46.** Photograph of the garden at Hamilton House, South Berwick, Maine, 1928. Paul J. Weber, photographer.

**47.** Photograph of the Blue Steps at Naumkeag, Stockbridge, Mass., 1996. Photograph © Richard Cheek for The Trustees of Reservations.

**48.** Photograph of the Moon Gate at Naumkeag, Stockbridge, Mass., 1996. Photograph © Richard Cheek for The Trustees of Reservations.

**49.** Photograph of children at Historic New England's Homeschool Program, Hamilton House, South Berwick, Maine, 2017. Photographer unknown.

**50.** Photograph of the garden at Graftonwood, Manchester, Mass. Frances Benjamin Johnston, photographer. Published in *Beautiful Gardens in America* by Louise Shelton (New York: Charles Scribner's Sons, 1924.)

**51.** Photograph of Aza in the garden, Lexington, Mass., 2019. Julia Sedykh, photographer.

**52.** Photograph of Richard C. Nylander in his garden, Portsmouth, N. H., 2019. Lorna Condon, photographer.

**53.** Photograph of Martine Georges at the Lyman Estate Greenhouses, Waltham, Mass., c. 2019. Photographer unknown.

**54.** Photograph of a family in the Lyman Estate Greenhouses, Waltham, Mass., 2017. Beth Oram, photographer.

### An Unexpected Story: Social Revolution and the Garden Club by Virginia Lopez Begg

PAGES 124–135

**1.** Souvenir book for the Horticultural Exhibition "Gardens on Parade" at the New York World's Fair 1939, operated by Hortus, Inc.

**2.** Cover of *Your Garden: Plan-Planting-Care* by Donald Gray (Akron, Ohio, and New York: Saalfield Publishing, 1935.)

**3.** *A Road Map of Rye, Greenwich, New Ca-*

naan, *Ridgefield* [Conn.] *& Bedford* [N. Y.]. Prepared for the Fourteenth Annual Meeting of the Garden Club of America, 1927. Drawn by M. C. Bridgman, 1927.

**4.** Cover of program for the *Annual Meeting Garden Club of America, June 14–15–16–17–1927.*

**5.** Title page of *Gardens of Colony and State*, compiled and edited by Alice G. B. Lockwood (New York: Charles Scribner's Sons for The Garden Club of America, 1931.)

**6–7.** Cover of and foreword from the *Conservation Guide*, compiled by the Conservation Committee of the Garden Club of America (New York: The Garden Club of America, 1939.)

**8.** Cover of *The Golden Age of American Gardens: Proud Owners, Private Estates, 1890–1940* by Mac Griswold and Eleanor Weller (New York: Harry N. Abrams in Association with the Garden Club of America, 1991.)

**9.** Photograph of a display at the 1937 Spring Flower Show, Mechanics Building, Boston. P. E. Genereux, photographer.

**10.** Photograph of a display at the Spring Flower Show, Mechanics Building, Boston, n.d. P. E. Genereux, photographer.

**11.** Cover of *Guide to the Spring Flower Exhibition of the Massachusetts Horticultural Society, Mechanics Building, March 17–21, 1931.*

**12.** Cover of the *Official Program of the 65th Annual Spring Flower Show, Boston, Mass.*, held at the Mechanics Building, March 23–28, 1936.

**13.** Ticket to the Massachusetts Horticultural Society's Spring Flower Show, Mechanics Building, Boston, March 18–23, 1946.

**14.** Ticket to the Massachusetts Horticultural Society's Spring Flower Show, Mechanics Building, Boston, March 9–15, 1952.

**15.** Photograph of the Flower Club of the Ebenezer Baptist Church, Boston, November 15, 1946. Photographer unknown.

**16.** Photograph of Mrs. Francis King and members of the Garden Club of Michigan in 1927. D. D. Spellman, photographer.

**17.** Title page from *Historic Gardens of Virginia*, compiled by the James River Garden Club; edited by Edith Tunis Sale (Richmond, Va.: The James River Garden Club, 1923.)

**18.** Photograph of the first prize winning entry in the International Flower Show, New York, 1935, designed by Mrs. Henry G. Vaughan [Elise Tyson Vaughan], owner of Hamilton House, South Berwick, Maine. Photographer unknown.

**19–22.** First Prize Award from the Rhode Island Federation of Garden Clubs, Inc., presented to Joanne Carpenter Landsteiner of Barrington, R. I., for her arrangement of gladiolus, beach grass, and forsythia root,

1967; Third and Second Prize Awards from the North Andover [Mass.] Garden Club, presented to Sarah Moore Field, 1930, 1933; Creativity Award from the National Council of State Garden Clubs, Inc., presented to Joanne Carpenter Landsteiner, 1994.

**23.** Photograph of a flower arrangement by Joanne Carpenter Landsteiner of Barrington, R. I., and Naples, Fla., n.d. Photographer unknown.

**24.** First Award from the Barrington [R. I.] Garden Club presented to Joanne Carpenter Landsteiner (Mrs. Ernest K. Landsteiner) for her arrangement of white gladiolus, n.d.

## Gifts and Loans

Historic New England is grateful to Richard Cheek for donating or lending the following items for use in this book. The items are identified either by the page on which they appear or by the chapter in which they appear and the illustration number within the chapter.

*Pages:* 1–2, 4, 8; *Reading the Garden:* 1–2, 9–10, 12–13, 14–15, 17–19, 22–25, 28–30, 32–33, 36–37, 39, 43–45, 48–49, 51, 56–57, 59–65, 66–71, 73, 75, 78–84, 88; *Great Expectations:* 1–3, 6, 7–14, 21, 25, 33, 38–43, 53–57, 58–59, 61, 64–65, 67–68, 75–76, 78; *Beyond the Garden Gate:* 2–3, 5, 7, 11, 13, 19, 21–22, 24, 27–28, 30–31, 35, 38–39, 41, 44–48, 51–52, 55–56; *Where Flowers Never Fade:* 43, 47–48; *An Unexpected Story:* 1, 17.

Historic New England is also grateful to the following individuals for lending items for use in this book. The items are identified by the page(s) on which they appear and the illustration number: Virginia Lopez Begg (pages 124:2, 132:16); Thomas G. Boss (page 6); Lorna Condon (pages 33:76–77, 35:85–87); Richard C. Nylander (pages 42:16, 66–67:77, 79–82); Kristin L. Servison (page 135:19, 21, 23–24); Judith B. Tankard (pages 19:16, 22:38, 26:52–54, 44–45:26).

## Index

Page numbers in *italics* indicate illustrations within the text. For complete information on individual images, see numbered references within Illustration Sources (pages 136–41).

Aesthetic Movement, 38
*American Estates and Gardens* (Ferree), 14, 21, *20–21*
*American Flower Garden, The* (Blanchan), *6*
*American Gardens* (Lowell), 14, *20*, 21, 70, 96

*American Homes and Gardens* (periodical), 14, *24*
American Society of Landscape Architects, 14
Anderson, Larz and Isabel, 96, *116–17*
anthropomorphic plants, 10, 38, 54, *55*
Appledore Island (Maine), *94*, 96
arbors, *24*, *41*, *55*, *67*, 69–70, *71*, *72–3*, *75*, *74–5*, *92–3*, *113*, *118–19*, *124*
architectural features in gardens. *See* arbors, bridges, fences, gates, greenhouses, pergolas, summer houses, treillage
*Architectural Record* (periodical), 96
Arlington (Mass.), 96, *106–7*
Arnold Arboretum (Harvard), 14
Arts and Crafts Movement, 13, 14. *See also* bungalows, *Craftsman, The* (periodical)
Asian gardens, 21, *21*
Austin, David, 67, *66–7*

Beal, Robert Washburn, 28, *28–9*
*Beautiful Gardens in America* (Shelton), 14, *19*, 96
benches, 9, 64, 70, *88–9*, *109*
*Better Homes and Gardens* (periodical), 96
*Better Homes and Gardens Book*, 15, *34–5*
*Bird Girl* (sculpture), 70
birdbaths, *55*, *66*, 84, *84*, *88–9*
birdhouses, 84, *85*
Blanchan, Neltje, *6*, 13
Blossom, Harold Hill, 29
Boston, 38, 60, 70, 95–7, 100–01, 130, *130–31*, 132, *132*. *See also* Spring Flower Show (Boston)
Boston Athenaeum, 96
Boston Woven Hose and Rubber Company, 60, *60*
Bowen, Henry, 96
Breck, Joseph, 38, 43
Breck's (nursery), 37–8, 67, *66*
bridges, *104–5*, *106–7*, *108*
Brighton (Mass.), 38
Brookline (Mass.), 4, 96, *114–15*, *116–17*
Brown, Lancelot "Capability," 95
Browne, Herbert W. C., 97
Budding, Edwin, 59
bulbs, 8, 38, *44–5*, 53, *53*
bungalows, 13, 14, 41
Burnett, Frances Hodgson, 32, *33*
Burpee, W. Atlee & Co. (seed company), *36*, 37, *45*, 50, 53

calendars. *See* garden calendars
catalogues, 9, *36*, 37–8, 49, 50, 60, *60–61*, 67, 69, 70
*Century Magazine, The*, 96
Charles C. Hart (seed company), 37, *49*
children and gardening, 31, *30–31*, 32, *32–3*, 38, 45, *45*, 59, 62, 68, 77, 84, *84;* in advertis-

ing, *30–31, 39, 47, 49, 63, 84;* gardening books for children, 32, *32–3*
Choate, Mabel, 97
chromolithography, 37–8, 50
Civil War, 37, 125
Codman Estate (Lincoln, Mass.), 96, *112–13*
Codman family, *74,* 96, *113*
Coffin, Marian, 14
Colonial Revival style, *12,* 13, 38, 41, 57, *56–7,* 70, 73, 80, *80,* 85, 88, 126
color in gardening, 13, 15, 17, *18–19, 26,* 38, 73, 96
*Colour in the Flower Garden* (Jekyll), 15, *26*
Comstock Ferre (seed company), 67, *66*
concrete, 70, 87, *87,* 89, *88–9*
conservation. *See* historic gardens (American), interest in; native plants
Constable, Stuart, *28–9*
Copeland, Robert, 17
*Country Life* (Copeland), 17
*Country Life* (English periodical), 14
*Country Life in America* (periodical), 14, 25, *24,* 96
*Craftsman, The* (periodical), 14, *24*

D. M. Ferry and Company, 46, *47*
Davidson, Charles Mowbray, *28–9*
Downing, Andrew Jackson, 17

Earle, Alice Morse, 13, *18–19*
École des Beaux-Arts (Paris), 14
Ely, Helena Rutherfurd, 13, *18,* 126
*English Flower Garden, The* (Robinson), 15
English gardens, 14–15, *15, 16,* 21, 26, *26–7,* 70, 95
estate gardens, 14–15, 17, 21, *20–21,* 23, *24,* 26, *27,* 43, 57, *56–7,* 69, 70, 73, 80, *80–81,* 95–7, *98–9, 104–5, 106–7, 108–9, 112–13, 114–15, 116–17. See also* formal gardens, *individual estates*

Farrand, Beatrix, 14
Faulkner Farm (Brookline, Mass.), 96
Featherstone, Donald "Don," 70
fences, *12,* 28, 32, 38, *41,* 69, 70, 80, *80–81*
Ferree, Barr, 14, 21, *20–21*
fertilizers, *10,* 38, *54–5,* 126
Fisher, Alvan, 95
flamingos (garden ornament), 9, 70, *90*
Flower Club of the Ebenezer Baptist Church, 132, *132*
flower gardening, *6, 8, 9,* 13, 14, 15, *18–19, 34, 36,* 37, 38, *39,* 45, *44–5,* 46, 50, 53, *52–3,* 67, *66–7,* 69, 73, 96, 125, 126–7, 130, *130–31,* 135, *134–5. See also* bulbs, flower shows, roses
flower shows, 127, 130, *130–31,* 135, *134–5*
flowerpots. *See* pots

Flushing (N. Y.), 126
formal gardens, 13, 14–15, *20–21, 23, 24,* 70, 73, *95–6, 108–11, 123,* 126. *See also* parterres, topiary, Victorian gardens
fountains, 9, *15, 23, 24,* 68, 69, 70, 72, 82, *82–3, 106, 116–17*
French gardens, 14, 21. *See also* formal gardens, parterres
Frick, Henry Clay, 70, *80–81*
fruit, 37, *43,* 50, *50–51,* 73, 95
fruit trees, 37, 95
furniture. *See* lawn furniture

*Garden & Home Builder* (periodical), *2,* 14
garden apparel, 9, 38
garden calendars, 13, 15, *16,* 17, 35
Garden Club of America (GCA), 126–7, 129, *128–9*
Garden Club of Michigan, 132, *132*
Garden Club of Philadelphia, 126
Garden Club of Virginia, 127, 132
garden clubs, 9, *124,* 125–35
garden furniture. *See* lawn furniture
garden gnomes, 70, *90–91*
garden hoses, 55, 60, *60*
garden literature, 13–15, *17–35,* 69–71, 96, 126–7, *128–9.* See also *individual titles;* women and gardening: gardening books and periodicals for women; children and gardening: gardening books for children
*Garden Magazine, The* (periodical), 14
*Garden of a Commuter's Wife, The* (Wright), 13, *18*
garden ornament, 10, 37, 38, 69–71, 87, 89, 90, *90–91.* See also birdbaths, birdhouses, flamingos (garden ornament), garden gnomes, garden sculpture, mirror globes, pots, St. Francis (garden ornament), sundials
garden photography, 14, 15, 70, 95–7, 122, *122–3,* 127
garden plans, *2,* 15, 17, *17,* 40–41, 69, 72, 95, *102–3;* for purchase, 28, *28–9,* 63, 70, 74, 75
garden sculpture, 9, *68,* 69, 70, *82–3,* 90, *90–91, 106–7, 109, 112–13, 116–17, 122–3,* 127. *See also* garden gnomes
garden tools, *2,* 9, 15, *30–31,* 37, 38, 60, *61, 66,* 69. *See also* garden hoses, lawn mowers, watering cans
*Gardens of Colony and State* (Garden Club of America), 127, *129*
*Gardens of Italy, The* (Latham), 23, *23*
gates, 9, *19, 43,* 68, 69, 70, 80, *80–81, 93, 121, 124*
gazebos. *See* summer houses
General Federation of Women's Clubs, 125
gnomes. *See* garden gnomes
Gothic Revival style, 70, 96, *110–11*
Gottscho, Samuel, 96
Greenaway, Kate, 38, 53
Greene, Gardiner, 95, *100–01*

greenhouses, 70, 78, *78–9,* 95, *105*
grottos, 82, *82*

Hales, John Groves, 95
Hamilton House (South Berwick, Maine), 97, *118–19,* 122
hammocks, 9, *64*
Hassam, Childe, *94,* 96
Henderson, Peter, 46, *46. See also* Peter Henderson & Co. (seed company)
Hewitt, Mattie Edwards, 14, 96
historic gardens (American), 9, 13, 14, 17, 25, 37, 70, 97, 126–7, 129, *129,* 132, *133*
Historic Garden Week (Virginia), 127, 132, *133*
historical garden styles. *See* Asian gardens, English gardens, French gardens, historical gardens (American), Italian gardens, Spanish gardens
hoses. *See* garden hoses
*House & Garden* (periodical), 14, *24,* 96
*House Beautiful, The* (periodical), *12,* 14, 22, 25, *24–5, 72,* 97
Hunnewell Estate (Wellesley, Mass.), 96, *108–9*

industry and gardening, 38, *46,* 54, *54–5,* 59, *58–9,* 60, *60–61, 64–5,* 70, *88–9,* 96, 125–7. *See also* catalogues, trade cards, *individual companies*
insects, 38, *54–5. See also* pesticides
*Island Garden, An* (Thaxter), 17, *94,* 96
Isles of Shoals (Maine), 94, *94,* 96
Italian gardens, 14, 21, 23, *22–3,* 70, 73, 96, *112–13*
*Italian Gardens* (Platt), 23, *23*
*Italian Villas and Their Gardens* (Wharton), *22,* 23

James River Garden Club (Virginia), *133*
Jekyll, Gertrude, 15, 26, *26*
Jerome B. Rice Company (seed company), *39, 46,* 54
Johnston, Frances Benjamin, 14, 96

Kent, William, 95
Kidder Estate. *See* Lilacs, The (Medford, Mass. estate)
Kidder, Thomas, 95
King, Louisa Yeomans, 132, *132*

*Ladies' Home Journal, The* (periodical), 14, *24,* 25, *28–9*
landscape architecture (profession), 9, 14–15, 23, 28, *28,* 57, 69, 75, 95, 97, 126–7, 129
*Landscape Gardening Book, The* (Tabor), 15, *18*

Langdon House (Portsmouth, N. H.), 80
Latham, Charles, 23
lawn furniture, 9, 10, 13, *28*, 38, *41*, 57, *57*, 62, *62–3*, 64, *64–5*, *68*, 69–70. See also benches, outdoor living rooms
lawn mowers, 9, 59, *58–9*
lawns, 38, 59, *58–9*, 70, 96
Lilacs, The (Medford, Mass. estate), 95, *98–9*
Lincoln (Mass.), 96, *112–13*
literature. See garden literature
Little and Browne (architectural firm), *81*, 97
Long Island (N. Y.), 126
Lord & Burnham Company (greenhouse manufacturer), 70, *79*
Lowell, Guy, 14, *20*, 21, 70, 96
Lyman Estate (Waltham, Mass.), 78, *78–9*, 95, *104–5*
Lyman, Theodore, 78, 95

manure. See fertilizers
Marr, T. E. and Sons (photography studio), 96
Massachusetts Horticultural Society, 125, *131*
Medford (Mass.), 95, *98–9*
mirror globes, 9, *97*
M'Mahon, Bernard, 13, 17
Mount Vernon, 57, *57*
Munstead Wood (Surrey, England estate), 15, 26, *26*

National Garden Clubs, 127
Native American imagery (advertising), *42*, *54*
native plants, 14–15, 26, 126–7, 129
Naumkeag (Stockbridge, Mass. estate), 97, *120–21*
New England gardens, 13, *28*, 37, 38, 43, *43*, 70, 78, *78–9*, 80, *80*, *94*, 95–7, *98–9*, *100–01*. See also *individual estates, individual cities*
New York State Federation of Garden Clubs, 126
New York World's Fair (1939), 124, *124*
nurseries, 9, 13, 15, 17, 35, 37, 38, 43, *42–3*, 67, *66*, 70, 127

*Old Time Gardens* (Earle), 17, *18*
Olmsted, Frederick Law, 14, 96
orchards. See fruit trees
ornament. See garden ornament
outdoor living rooms, 38, 62, *62–3*, 64, *64–5*. *See also* arbors, greenhouses, lawn furniture, patios, summer houses

Paris, Frances Johnston, 126
Parrish, Maxfield, 23, *22*, 46, *47*
parterres, *20–21*, 24, 95, 96. *See also* formal gardens
paths, 9, *17*, *20–21*, 22, *26–7*, 69, *79*, 88, 96, 97, *108*

patios, *62–3*, *64–5*
patriotism and gardening, 31, *30–31*, *56–7*, *126–7*. *See also* Colonial Revival style, historic gardens (American)
pergolas, *23*, *41*, 65, 69–70, 73, *72–3*, *87*, *92–3*, *102*, *112*, *123*, *129*
pesticides, 38, *54–5*
Peter Henderson & Co. (seed company), 46, *46*, *56–7*
photography. See garden photography
plans. See garden plans
Platt, Charles, 23, *23*, 96
Portsmouth (N. H.), 95, *102–3*
pots, 38, *23*, 69, 70, 71, *71*, 87, *86–7*, *88–9*, *109*, *112*, *116*
Potter, Joseph F., 96
Potter's Grove (Arlington, Mass. estate), 96, *106–7*
Pratt, Henry Cheever, 95

Robinson, William, 14–15, 26
rock gardens, 13, 127
roses, 13, *19*, *34*, *36*, 53, *52*, 67, *66–7*, *102*, *131*
Roseland Cottage (Woodstock, Conn.), 96, *110–11*
Rundlet–May House (Portsmouth, N. H.), 95, *102–3*
rustic style, 77, 80, *80*, *108*

Salmon, Robert, 95
Schinkel, Karl Friedrich, 57
Schlesinger, Barthold and Mary McBurney, 96
Schlesinger Estate. See Southwood (Brookline, Mass. estate)
sculpture. See garden sculpture
seasonal gardening, 15, *18–19*, *31*, *35*, 37, 43, 53, *53*. *See also* garden calendars
*Secret Garden, The* (Burnett), 32, *33*
seeds, *31*, *36*, 37–8, *39*, 43, 45, *44–5*, 46, *46–7*, 49, *48–9*, 50, *50*, 54, 60, *66*, 126. *See also* catalogues, *individual seed companies*
Sedgwick, Mabel Cabot, 13, 14
Shakers (religious sect), 38, 45, *44*
Shelton, Louise, 14, *18–19*, 96
Shipman, Ellen, 14
South Berwick (Maine), 97, *118–19*
Southwood (Brookline, Mass. estate), 96, *114–15*
Spanish gardens, 14, 21, *21*
Sprague, Charles, 96
Spring Flower Show (Boston), 130, *130–31*
sprinklers, 60, *60*
statuary. See garden sculpture
Stebbins, Nathaniel Livermore, 96
Steele, Fletcher, *29*, 97
Stevens, Beatrice, *53*, *53*
Stockbridge (Mass.), 97, *120–21*
suburbs, 13, 14, *18*, 25, 38, 62, *62–3*, 69, 70, 126

summer houses, 9, *23*, 69, 70, 77, *76–7*, *98*, *106*, *108–9*, *118*
sundials, 9, 13, *18*, *19*, *43*, 53, *53*, 69, 71, 84, *88–9*, *93*, *92–3*

Tabor, Grace, 15, *18*
*Taylor's Weekend Gardening Guides* (series), 13, 15, 35, *35*
Thaxter, Celia, 17, *94*, 96
tools. See garden tools
topiary, 15, *89*, 96, *108–9*, *116–17*
trade cards, 10, 37, *39*, 46, 54, *54–5*, 59, *59*, 60
treillage, 69, 70, *74–5*
trellis. See arbors, pergolas, treillage
Tyson, Elise. See Vaughan, Elise (*née* Tyson)
Tyson, Emily, 96–7

Underwood, Loring, 71, 144
urns. See pots

Vale, The (Waltham, Mass. estate). See Lyman Estate (Waltham, Mass.)
Van Rensselaer, Mariana Griswold, 14, 21
vases. See pots
Vaughan, Elise (*née* Tyson), 97
vegetable gardening, 9, *30*, 31, *31*, 37, 38, 43, 45, *44–5*, 46, 49, *48–9*, 54, *54–5*, 60, 95
Victorian gardens, 13, *17*, 37–8, 57, 70, 95–7, *97*, *105–9*, 125, 126
Victory Gardens, 31, *30–31*

W. Atlee Burpee & Co. (seed company). See Burpee, W. Atlee & Co. (seed company)
Waltham (Mass.), 95, *104–5*
Washington, George, 37, 57
water features, 13, *20*, *23*, 26, *39*, 65, *68*, 69, 70, 71, 72, 78, 82, *82–3*, 96, *104–5*, *106–7*, *112*, *116–17*. See also birdbaths, fountains, garden hoses, grottos, sprinklers
watering cans, *1*, *32*, *47*, 60, *61*
Weber, Paul, 97
Weld (Brookline, Mass. estate), 96, *116–17*
Wellesley (Mass.), 96, *108–9*
Wharton, Edith, *22*, 23
White Flower Farm (nursery), 67, *66*
*Wild Garden, The* (Robinson), 14–15, 26
Wilder, Louise Beebe, 15
*Woman's Hardy Garden, A* (Ely), 17, *18*, 126
women and gardening, 13–15, 17, *18–19*, *40–41*, 59, 96, 111, 124–7; women in garden advertising, *10*, *40–41*, 53, *55*, *56–7*, *58–9*, *63*, *64*; gardening books and periodicals for women, 13, *18–19*. See also garden clubs
Woodstock (Conn.), 96, *110–11*
World War I, *30*, *31*, 127
World War II, 31, *31*
Wright, Mabel Osgood, 13

## Editor's Acknowledgments

I am deeply indebted to the following for their great contributions to this book:

*Chief perfectionist and production manager:* Lorna Condon. *Endlessly creative series book designer:* Julia Sedykh. *Photographer:* Chloe Schoppmeyer. *Cataloguers:* Mary Beth Dunhouse and Kathy Kiefer. *Text editor:* Dorothy A. Clark. *Indexer:* R. Tripp Evans. *Legal advisor:* Jeff Johnson of WilmerHale LLP. *Printers:* Jay Stewart, Steve Jaquint, and Tom Longval. *Home team:* my wife, Betsy, and my son, Dan.

## About the Contributors

**Judith B. Tankard** is an art historian specializing in landscape history. She taught at the Landscape Institute, Harvard University, for more than twenty years and is the author or co-author of ten books, including *Beatrix Farrand: Private Gardens, Public Landscapes*, which was named an Honor Book by Historic New England.

**Richard C. Nylander** is curator emeritus of Historic New England where he studied all aspects of its holdings—from decorative arts and household objects to historic houses and landscapes. He is an internationally recognized expert on historic wallpaper and has written extensively on the subject.

**Alan Emmet** is the author of *So Fine a Prospect: Historic New England Gardens*. She has written articles for many magazines, including *Horticulture*, *Garden Design*, and *House & Garden* where she wrote for twenty years. She has also been a consultant in landscape history for several organizations.

**Virginia Lopez Begg** is a landscape historian and author of many articles about women and the American landscape. She curated the 1993 exhibition, *A Room of One's Own: The American Woman Garden Writer, 1900–1940*, at the Arthur and Elizabeth Schlesinger Library on the History of Women in America, Harvard University.

All of the contributors maintain home gardens.

FRONT COVER: Back cover of catalogue, *1897 Childs Rare Flowers, Vegetables, and Fruits* (Floral Park, N. Y.: John Lewis Childs) and illustration from catalogue, *Manual of Everything for the Garden, 1885* (New York: Peter Henderson).

FRONT FLAP: Cover of catalogue, *Manual of Everything for the Garden, 1885* (New York: Peter Henderson).

FRONT INSIDE COVER: *The Grange Lincoln Sept [18]98.* Watercolor of the Codman Estate, Lincoln, Mass., by Sarah Fletcher Bradlee Codman.

BACK COVER: Trade card for Bulldog Garden Hose (Boston: Boston Woven Hose and Rubber, n.d.).

BACK FLAP: Decoration from catalogue, *L. L. May & Co., 1898* (St. Paul, Minn.: L. L. May).

BACK INSIDE COVER: *Garden Sketch for Mrs. C. Oliver Iselin* by Loring Underwood, Landscape Architect, n.d. Probably an unbuilt proposal for the Iselin garden in Providence, R. I.

Published by
HISTORIC NEW ENGLAND
141 Cambridge Street
Boston, Massachusetts 02114
www.HistoricNewEngland.org

Distributed in North America by
CASEMATE IPM
1950 Lawrence Road, Havertown, PA 19083, USA
Telephone: 1 610 853 9131
E-mail: casemate@casematepublishers.com

And the rest of the world by
CASEMATE UK
The Old Music Hall
106–108 Cowley Road, Oxford, OX4 1JE, UK
Telephone: 1 610 853 9131
E-mail: trade@casematepublishers.co.uk

First Edition 2019
Library of Congress Cataloging-in-Publication Data is available from the Library of Congress.
ISBN: 978-0-9890598-4-8

Book and cover design by Julia Sedykh Design
Printed in the United States by Puritan Capital, Hollis, New Hampshire
Bound in the United States by Superior Packaging and Finishing, Braintree, Massachusetts